Law and Philosophy of Language

Academic legal production, when focusing on the study of law, generally grasps this concept on the basis of a reference to positive law and its practice. This book differs clearly from these analyses and integrates the legal approach into the philosophy of normative language, philosophical realism and pragmatism. Not only is the aim to place the examination of law in the immanence of its practice, but also to take note of the fact that legal enunciation must be taken seriously. In order to arrive at this analysis, it is necessary to go beyond traditional perspectives and to base the reflection on an investigation of the conditions for enunciating law in our democracies. Thus, this analysis offers a renewal of the ethics inherent in the action of jurists and an original reflection on the role of certain legal tools such as concepts, categories, or "provisions". In this sense, the work nourishes its originality not only by the transversality of its approach, but also by the will to situate legal thought in concrete forms of its implementation.

The book will be essential reading for academics working in the areas of legal theory, legal philosophy and constitutional theory.

Pascal Richard is Lecturer in Public Law at the University of Toulon, France.

Routledge Research in Constitutional Law

This series features thought-provoking and original scholarship on constitutional law and theory. Books explore key topics, themes and questions in the field with a particular emphasis on comparative studies. Where relevant, titles will engage with political and social theory, philosophy and history in order to offer a rounded analysis of constitutions and constitutional law. Series Editor: David Marrani

Available titles in this series include:

Constitutional Law, Religion and Equal Liberty
The Impact of Desecularization
Azin Tadjdini

Kant, Global Politics and Cosmopolitan Law
The World Republic as a Regulative Idea of Reason
Claudio Corradetti

Diversity of Law in the United Arab Emirates
Privacy, Security and the Legal System
Kristin Kamøy

Sovereignty, Civic Participation, and Constitutional Law
The People versus the Nation in Belgium
Edited by Brecht Deseure, Raf Geenens and Stefan Sottiaux

Law and Philosophy of Language
Ordinariness of Law
Pascal Richard

For more information about this series, please visit: www.routledge.com/Routledge-Research-in-Constitutional-Law/book-series/CONSTLAW

Law and Philosophy of Language

Ordinariness of Law

Pascal Richard

Routledge
Taylor & Francis Group
LONDON AND NEW YORK

First published 2021
by Routledge
2 Park Square, Milton Park, Abingdon, Oxon OX14 4RN

and by Routledge
605 Third Avenue, New York, NY 10158

Routledge is an imprint of the Taylor & Francis Group, an informa business

British Library Cataloguing-in-Publication Data
A catalogue record for this book is available from the British Library

Library of Congress Cataloging-in-Publication Data
A catalog record has been requested for this book

ISBN: 978-0-367-65562-4 (hbk)
ISBN: 978-0-367-65564-8 (pbk)
ISBN: 978-1-003-13010-9 (ebk)

DOI: 10.4324/9781003130109

Typeset in Galliard
by Taylor & Francis Books

Contents

Illustrations

Figure

Tables

Introduction

By using this reference to the "ordinariness of the law" we can give the appearance of giving in to a facility of language and thus mask an ambiguity that would be inherent in our discourse: the rhetorical ornament would then become the bedrock of equivocation. Indeed, what is the nature of this ordinary that will be the core of our discourse? Is it the ordinary of the interpretation of law? Is it the ordinary of its implementation? The ordinary of its creation? Similarly, what law are we talking about? Is it a disciplinary field? Is it a specific discourse? Positive law? Will the law be an opportunity, through a metonymic shift, to deal with the norm, the legal rule or the legal utterance?

The aim of this book is to synthetisize in its own way, these various questions and to offer an original response to the question of the nature of law and its effective integration into a social space. The challenge lies, in this way, in our willingness to question some dichotomies (law and language, effectiveness and validity, meaning and significance, norms and law, normativism and realism) which are strongly rooted in legal thinking and which now seem to have to be overcome because they are so many resistances to the legal phenomenon itself. Very often, thought, when enlever le "it is" constructed on the basis of such opposition, avoids grasping the very nature of this dichotomy and its consequences for the object that is to be thought about: the semblance of this dialectic obscures its essence or reality. What makes the ordinary of law a screen is thus the screen on which it is projected in legal language: its representation. For Kelsen, for example, the norm can be understood either as a simply thought norm or as a valid norm. The simply thought norm can be hypothetical (this is the case of the fundamental norm) or an effective norm which is merely the representation in awareness of the valid norm.[1]

The reason why we have relied – in this book – on this idea of the ordinary of law is to evoke the ultimately simple and pragmatic – but always hidden – notion that the extraordinary of the legal phenomenon (its "magic" capacity to generate normative effects) exists in legal discourse only as the ordinary of a discourse that

1 On a remarkable analysis of this distinction between lived and thought norms: L. PASSERINI-GLAZEL, "Les normes vécues et les normes simplement pensées *noema* déontique et expérience normative dans Kelsen, Weber, Petrażycki and Weinberger," in *Sociologie du droit* (2018), 1.

DOI: 10.4324/9781003130109-1

is rationally as ordinary as any other. Indeed, whatever is stated is irremediably only a "saying" and to answer for it from the ordinary of the situation in which it is expressed.

We do not refute the idea that some contexts are singular. However, these usually remain contexts linked to enunciation. What is ordinary is that in some way or another "I" is enunciating something. What is "extraordinary" is finally the ordinary of social life and the always singular way supprimer actors agree in it and generate normativity.

It is then a question of accounting for a reconciliation in the same "flesh" of enunciations and statements, objectivity and subjectivity as well as immanence and transcendence that haunt legal discourse in the form of duplicating reality that can only generate ghosts within legal thinking. The ordinariness of law is that there is no other world than the one in which the legal operator finds himself immersed and where he must assume the unimpeachable part of enunciation that is present in his utterance. Everyone should be responsible for their statements from the place where they make them. It is only on this condition that an ethics of legal discourse develops and not just a flat and uniform social morality.

It is obvious, of course, that this empiricism – or realistic pragmatism – does not obscure the fact that in *this* world the arguments that legal statements carry in the form of legal propositions seem to belong to a specific rationality and a singular logic (modal, ethical, etc.). Indeed, we need a screen on which to project our legal pretensions and make the film of law. If the mechanism is ordinary, the film can be extraordinary. This differentiation between the diegetic space of a discourse and its space of enunciation is classic and is manifested in the various methods that make it possible, with varying degrees of success, to show this gap and to link one space to another.

Positive law thus closes itself off to its enunciation by presenting it as heterogeneous: as political, factual, moral, etc. The truth of the law would be inherent in its own order. This closure is even the hallmark of the definition of legal positivism: law is then what law considers to be law. The status of the truth of a discourse in this perspective always takes the form of the ideology that makes one never really know what one is doing. This ideology does not so much confirm the presence of real ignorance as of a bad faith which that haunts analyses and testifies to a readiness to avoid the embarrassments of the ordinary in favor of the apparent certainties that are inherent in practical and operational discourses. In this hypothesis, the ordinariness of the law is obscured by the presence of a habit (a "habit of action," i.e., a belief according to pragmatic approaches). The common distinction between faith and belief can be found here in a secularised form: true faith borne of doubt is an ever-repeated struggle against doubt, whereas belief is inscribed in an apparent certainty: it expresses a certain resting of thought. Belief in the discourse of law – which happens to be supprimer only a habit in a pragmatic approach – operates, in this way, to the detriment of a critical faith in what law could be. Belief in law ideologically erases the necessarily fragile faith *in* law. The ordinary understood in this way is necessarily ethical, because it expresses resistance to the supprimer all too easy slope of belief: the awareness of a difference and a gap between the *doxa* and *the epistèmê, one* might say.... Between opinions and absolute certainty in a habit there is obvie: the incredibly fragile ordinary of a "form of life."

Thus, truth, rationality and values are generally separated in the legal discourse inherent in positive law.

Truth apprehended in the classical form of correspondence engenders, in essence, a duality between an object and what it refers to and as such must correspond. The truth of supprimer law would therefore be found in its reference or denotation, and each person, depending on what he or she "is," will then construct this correspondence, which is always fallacious (in morality, in a transcendence, in a factual reality, in a practice … we find here the recurring idea in legal discourse of the presence of "sources of law") because it is inscribed, from the outset, in the prison of a language in which the sign will perpetually be the tomb of the thing. Rationality, for its part, will be apprehended: either as the discovery of a general law, or as the discovery of regularities.... The law will then, for example, be renewed to the law of the validity of the norm (which would thus only be the *analogy of* causality) or reduced to the discovery of a series of regularities that will have to be renewed – possibly by abduction – to a meaning. These are the various most influential schools of legal theory. The "good" – or morality – as only the order of social utility of law or by the attachment to principles that are nothing but a disguise of the law of values that positive law rejects and dismisses – more or less well and more or less easily, as the contemporary influence of a certain "neo-constitutionalism" shows.

Finally, the most faithful approach to this ordinary that we are calling to rediscover is the one that apprehends law or rule as a tool in the ordinary of the world. A tool that would be at our fingertips: a compass or a ruler. A way of orienting ourselves in this world by taking stock of what is the particular way in which law appears in the world. The phenomenological approach is thus able to perceive that it is in the ordinariness of its appearance and its donation to consciousness that it offers not an access to the world, but a rationality to the implementation of our form of life. The law regulates the world and the world gives the norm. To follow the rule is in this respect only to give a reason for a cause in order to provide ourselves with a tool to judge the regularity of our actions.

Let us add that in the three-stranded rope – to use a famous formula – that form the mind, the body and the world, language is of essential importance. It is language that informs the whole and is, as such, fully our "form of life." It is impossible to escape from it, even if it offers, through its infinite resources, many illusions and desirable "backgrounds." It is thus enough to speak long enough to seem to give coherence to our discourse. In this respect, legal doctrine clearly gives meaning to legal statements: the discourse on law is intended to make explicit "a" meaning of the discourse of law. It offers the mind the rest of a habit and the oblivion for a time of reflection on the ordinariness of a practice.

Language is thus *in the* world and legal language is only one of its operational forms. Law is a discourse that clearly has a function, and, in this sense, it works to build part of a specialised sub-system inherent in our world. It works towards a function of legitimising and receiving social expectations: it helps to generate trust and belief and to make it possible to deal with expectations. In the form of legal policy, it also performs a function of decision-making and guidance of conduct, in the form of legal command.

Our purpose is not to develop a new and umpteenth demonstration of the conventional nature of language or legal language: in our view, and in accordance with the complex determination of a "life form," this approach is hemiplegic, as some ordinary language specialists have demonstrated. We are aware that the "grammar" in which our normativities are taken is not of this conventional type, but is embedded in a much more complex relationship to our "*life form*" of talking and social animals.

This book, therefore, seeks to examine some aspects of this ordinary grammar that is masked by legal ideology. As such, it will cross-reference various epistemological experiences that make up the lawyer's ordinary and that he often – because of the ordinary of his practice – discards without any real awareness of them: prisoner of this internal point of view that blinds us to its vanishing point. Concepts," "categories," the distinction between the "fundamental" and the "important," "dispositions," "dispositional realism," or the difference between "subjects of statements" and "subjects of enunciations," "philosophy of ordinary language" and "scepticism," "ethics" and the necessary ethics of reasonable belief will all be boundaries that will delimit our stay within the ordinariness of a practice to which we are necessarily invited.

The first chapter of this book deals specifically with the way in which law and politics are articulated in the enunciation of the French constitutional judge. It focuses on an examination of a recent decision handed down during the recent period of health emergency. During this very singular situation, which brings legal discourse to the limit, an ordinary that the ideology inherent in constitutional justice generally masks is manifested with great force – and with extreme obviousness. It is a question of showing – and demonstrating – the presence of an irrefutable part of enunciation in the statement of the constitutional judge. The rationality of an argument taken to its limits reveals the factual conditions inherent in the enunciation itself and should give rise to an ethics dedicated to this practice. It is here that the ordinary facts of the case impose themselves on the judges' reasoning.

The next chapter deals with the study of the development of a legal category. The category of "fundamental rights" has thus become pre-eminent in legal discourse. Indeed, it conveys an axiological legitimacy that reinforces the ideology of our modern rule of law. However, when this category is viewed through the prism of a conceptual analysis, it appears that it expresses not so much what is fundamental as what is important. This difference offers a new perspective on the ordinary use of this legal category. What is important is precisely the maintenance of this ordinary that gives density to the form of life regulated by the law. Under the mask of a search for a basis on which to present the ordinariness of a form of life. It is the ordinariness of a legal category and its rhetorical use that will be at the heart of our reflection.

Chapter 3 deals with the validity of the administrative judge's creations. This creative work is generally apprehended only on the basis of a truncated conception of validity. It seems to us that a more comprehensive conception of the validity of legal statements is not well understood. This question is important because the French administrative judge has been the creator of "administrative law" from the outset: he regularly renews it on the basis of "definitions" of "concepts" or "notions." These are conceptual elements which appear to him to be necessary for the performance of his office. In accordance with this contentious reality, he finds himself at a crossroads between a pragmatic legitimisation linked to the realism of his mission and a legitimisation induced by the respect of the formal validity of these decisions. This duality manifests an ambivalence of validity understood according to a classical definition as existence (or as the counterpart of existence in the legal order). It is this ambivalence which will be understood in this chapter from the perspective of legal logic. In this third chapter the ordinary ideology of the French administrative judge will be examined. This ideology – when one accepts its hold consciously or involuntarily – implies the impossibility of being able to criticise legal creations. It is this "logical trap" that usually works that will be at the heart of this chapter.

Chapter 4 will be dedicated studying the meaning of fault. This meaning seems to condition the ordinary functioning of the law. It seems to be the essential theme from which the law develops. In this sense, it forms the necessary background for the understanding of various legal concepts that share a family resemblance with fault. Guilt, fault and liability thus seem to find meaning in the field of law only within a theme that is the ordinary of law.

Chapter 5 deals specifically with the influence of dispositional concepts. We will wager that the expression of a disposition that appears as regularity and that is articulated in a field of relations offers to show the form of life that is inherent in man. The concepts are then normative, because they respond to this inherent disposition of what man is as spoken. Therefore, normativity itself is elucidated by this disposition would be specific to our form of life. Normativity would account for human reality and would be actualised in the form of various regularities. This question of normativity would only reflect the causal dynamic force of certain human and social dispositions. This normativity would be intrinsic to a field and could, however, appear as a law. It would not be a priori, but could be deduced a posteriori from, for example, an axiomatisation of regularities discovered in the course of an investigation. Moreover, this investigation carried out within the framework of the law is inherent in the use of language. Legal concepts are thus "dispositional" concepts that highlight the reciprocal and updated action of various provisions. It is for this reason that they are normative. In this short text that forms Chapter 5, the ordinary of normativity will be developed.

In Chapter 6 it is discrimination that is at work in Professor A. Conte's thinking. A tale that will be studied. In the work inherent in this reflection, which relates to the work of the great Italian professor (and which mainly concerns the study of the philosophy of normative language) seems to manifest the impossibility of relating certain elements. It is, in this way, the impossibility of fully relating two series that presents themselves as the ordinariness of our relationship to the world. The ordinary that forms our reality would only be the ordinary of this failure and non-reporting.

Finally, in Chapter 7 what is examined is the ordinariness of our commitments within social normativity. It is then a question of examining the specific way in which we relate to these forms of life that involve our sociability. It will be necessary in this respect to understand the nature of this agreement and the place of criteria and concepts in this adherence.

All in all, what the author wants in this book is to give readers the possibility of having certain milestones at their disposal in order to fully measure the influence of the ordinary. That is the flesh of our world and the heart of our life is paradoxically the very thing whose influence can no longer be perceived. The idea that the ordinary is ultimately the intuition of the real is played with the ordinary in the legal field. A way for the legal experience to take hold of itself in its own time – to formulate this experience in the form of a Bergson-like statement. In the block that legal experience seems to constitute in this way, what manifests itself is a constant resistance that is always concealed. Bergson's famous demonstration of duration is well known: "My memory is there, pushing something from the past into the present. My state of mind, as I move along the road of time, continually swells with the time it picks up; it snowballs with itself, so to speak."[2]

A similar perception is manifested with legal experience when it is understood in its duration. However, this ordinary duration of experience is not retained by attention and is masked in favor of the illusory block that would be the experience of law. The reflections of a current philosophy of mind promoted by Daniel Dennett seem to tend towards an identical demonstration. The certainty of an experience described in the first person would be illusory and would only account for the presence of a mask placed on the moving of a pure life that would be devoid of point of view:

> The flow of consciousness is cluttered with an endless stream of associations. And as each fugitive occupant of the most influential position leaves room for his or her successors, any effort to end this disorderly parade and to control the details of the associations only generates a new deluge of evanescent states, and so on. Coalitions of themes and projects can succeed in monopolising attention for a useful and extremely productive period, postponing possible disgressions long enough, and creating the fiction of a permanent self or ego taking over the whole operation.[3]

Being aware of the legal phenomenon's uniqueness would thus be a double illusion: on the one hand, that of the block of legal experience and, on the other hand, that of a "point of view" on this experience. The ordinariness of this experience would ultimately be summed up in the ordinariness of the project and the coalition; i.e., the theme that is formed at a certain point in the movement of life and on which, ordinarily, life agrees through us (i.e., beyond the apparent illusion of a point of view as stated in the first person). With the ordinary, it is thus the uniqueness of legal experience that is at issue – or more precisely the

2 H. BERGSON, *L'évolution créatrice,* Chapter 1 "The Evolution of Life. Mechanism and purpose," PUF, Paris, 1907.

3 D.C. DENNETT, *De beaux rêves: Obstacles philosophiques à une science de la conscience,* Gallimard, Paris, 2005, pp. 279–280.

questioning of the latter as likely to form a block. In this sense, we have tried to show in this book how under the "concepts" and "legal categories" that are usually accepted, it is the ordinariness of adherence and agreement to criteria that is hidden (or the oblivion of the dispositional aspects of these concepts). We have also sought to make it clear that this attention to the ordinary of law also implies a singular ethics that must be attentive to the duration of this ordinary of legal experience for the conscience.

1 The constitutional judge to the test of transgression

The example of the decision of March 26, 2020[1]

The Constitutional Council's decision of March 26, 2020 (Decision No. 799-DC) is for some the expression of a scandal[2] or it could be the manifestation of a stumbling block in the action by the French constitutional judge.[3] In either event, the constitutional judge decided not to respect the Constitution.

The facts are known. It was a question of examining the constitutionality of an organic law, the sole article of which stated:

> in order to deal with the consequences of the covid-19 virus epidemic, the time limits mentioned in articles 23–4, 23–5 and 23–10 of Ordinance No. 58–1067 of 7 November 1958 on the organic law on the Constitutional Council are suspended until 30 June 2020.

This article thus suspends the three-month period during which the Council of State and the Court of Cassation are required to rule on the transmission to the Council of a priority question of constitutionality. According to Article 46 of the Constitution:

1 Thanks to Christian Dubuis Santini and Lorenzo Passerini Glazel who each in their own way offered me their signifiers to teach me how to hear better.

2 A social enunciation by transforming itself into a "right" ignores the instance of the enunciation, which then appears as the grain of sand that will give consistency to our scepticism. A perfect illustration of this can be found in the Orestie. In this tragedy the grain of sand takes the form of a stone: the one that will allow Athena to vote. What turns language into decision is always a stumbling block and a scandal (*Proskomma*). To quote some who very quickly became scandalised or were "surprised" by this decision and without wishing to be exhaustive: J.E. Gicquel, R. Letteron, or V. Champeil-Desplats, "Le Conseil constitutionnel face à lui-même," *La revue des droits de l'homme*, April 2020. Clearly, this situation seems to be deteriorating in view of the reactions of part of the doctrine to the decision n°2020–843 QPC of May 28, 2020.

3 N. Boulic, "'Tu sais ne pas être injuste': Justice et procès dans les Euménides d'Eschyle," *Criminocorpus*, "Théâtre et Justice: autour de la mise en scène des *Criminels* de Ferdinand Bruckner par Richard Brunel," *Justice et théâtre: d'une fondation commune à la confrontation de deux paroles en crise*,http://journals.openedition.org/criminocorpus/2121 (accessed March 25, 2020).

DOI: 10.4324/9781003130109-2

> The law to which the Constitution confers the nature of organic laws shall be voted and amended under the following conditions: The draft or proposal may not be submitted to the deliberation and vote of the Assemblies on first reading until the deadlines set in the third paragraph of Article 42 have expired. However, if the accelerated procedure has been initiated under the conditions provided for in Article 45, the draft or proposal may not be submitted to the deliberations of the first meeting to which it is referred before the expiry of a period of fifteen days after its submission.

The Council of Ministers adopted the draft organic law on March 18, 2020. On this date, the government initiated the fast-track procedure on this text and it was tabled in the Senate. From March 19, the upper chamber examined it in committee and then in public session. The Senate voted on the bill at first reading 24 hours after it was tabled, thereby violating Article 46 of the Constitution. However, the Constitutional Court, in a spectacularly lapidary manner, merely stated that: "In view of the particular circumstances of the case, there is no reason for judge that this organic law was adopted in violation of the rules of procedure provided for in Article 46 of the Constitution." This analysis is particularly surprising in the light of what is generally presented as an abstract control on the relationship between norms.[4]

This decision illustrates various ambivalences that are linked to the enunciation of the law by the judge and that the health crisis offers to see in full light today. More precisely, this scandal shows, in its own way, the impossible catch-up – in the formulation of the law – between the subject of the statement and the subject of the enunciation[5]. This is a performative paradox in which the constitutional judge enunciates something and does something different from what he enunciates. It is this screen between *saying it* (the legal statement) and *doing it* (the legal enunciation) that we are going to question.

This decision will thus be the subject of three developments: the first concerns the positioning of the legal problem and the specific nature of the constitutional judge's enunciation (I). Following THIS demonstration, we will attempt to *show* the logic of the performative paradox that seems to us supprimer present in the constitutional judge's analysis. It will be a matter of representing the limits and the proximities inherent in the dimensions of enunciation and enunciation in the legal and political fields through the intermediary of topological thought (II). Finally,

4 On this question of the relationship between law and fact in the constitutional process: J.-J. PARDINI, *Le juge constitutionnel et le fait en Italie,* PUAM, Aix, Marseille, 2002.

5 B. LATOUR, "Notes breves sur l'écologie du droit saisie comme une énonciation," in *Cosmopolitiques: pratiques cosmopolitiques du droit, Cahiers théoriques pour l'écologie politique*, 8, L'Aube, Paris, 2004, pp. 34–40. The question we must ask ourselves is: how can we find the links between the different planes of enunciation, despite the constant discrepancy introduced by all the continuous dispatches that dislocate the continuity of words and deeds? Or, if you will how can we get back up the slope that has been constantly descended by the enunciative disengagements? (*op. cit.*, p. 35).

we will show how the Council could manage to justify what it does in the light of what it says in an ethic of its re-examined function (III).

I The nature of the enunciation of the constitutional judge: A performative paradox

In the decision of the constitutional court, the presence of a screen between what is stated in law and the act of enunciation that makes that statement (A) is thus apparent. This distinction makes it necessary to deal with the validity of the enunciation in a specific way, starting from a clarification of the pragmatic validity concept. (B).

A The gap between the legal statement and the legal enunciation

In an obvious but always hidden way, positive law – the positive statement validated as a right from the law – struggles to recover the part of the enunciation it is based on in terms of its meaning. The utterance acts as a screen the film of legal claims is projected on but supprimer by its nature would "screen" the reality of these claims.[6] This distortion is known and the jurist speaks of "legal qualification." In the legal field, this truth is expressed in many ways: the gap between the Sein and the *Sollen, the* fact and the law, the text and its meaning, the intelligence and the will, the internal point of view and the external point of view. In this dichotomy, what gets lost is the subject that states and lays down the legal proposition,[7] and what will be expressed this time *positively* is the preponderance of the *recognition of* a thing over the impossible *knowledge of the* thing "in itself." The legal

6 The aim here will be to report, albeit in a slightly different way, on an effect of what jurists conceive more easily by means of the classic opposition between "normativism" (which views the legal order as closed in on itself based on the distinction between existence and validity) and "realism" (which considers, for its part, that the legal statement must be open to the experience of a meaning that is itself likely to appear not in an act of intelligence – finding a right that is "already there" – but in an act of will). To name only the US realists, see also M.P. GOLDING, "Realism and Functionalism in the Legal Thoughts of Felix S. Cohen" (1981) *Cornell Law Quarterly* 66 (1032); K. LLEWELLYN, *Jurisprudence. Realism in Theory and Practice*, Routledge, New York, 2008.

7 This specialty language by its nature expresses an oversight of the position of the utterance, it is all in the inherent form of its utterance. It is thus constructed with regard to the foreclosure of any subject of the utterance. This foreclosure is countered by a certain empirical reading of the law. In this perspective: É. MILLARD, *Théorie du droit*, Dalloz, 2006. Professor Millard quotes Jérôme Frank, (*Court son Trial*, Princeton University Press, New York, 1949) who developed the famous formula that can account for the jurisdictional decision $D=PxS$. In this formula (P) corresponds to the personality of the judge and (S) to the stimuli. Millard develops this formula as follows: AC=D because N (an act of concretization is presented as a decision because of the presence of a norm). Moreover, this norm is analysed as follows $PxS \Rightarrow N$. The stimuli are understood as follows: $S = S(f) + S(cf) + S(inf)$ in this formula $S(f)$ corresponds to formalised sources of enunciations; $S(cf)$ to conformalised sources (sources to which one conforms) and $S(inf)$ *to* informal sources such as ideology.

statement that recognises the valid presence of an occult norm masks the knowledge of the legal operator's action. Professor Amselek spoke admirably of this need to place the acts of speech of the *jurisditeurs* within a certain horizon. The latter never "say" only the legal regulation; they also "say" what they are doing.[8] This discrepancy implies examining the decision that is important to us for specificity in the constitutional judge's logic within the philosophy of normative language.

B Taking into account a pragmatic validity.

In positive law, two dimensions seem to be inherent in the relationship between law and language. In fact, if it is impossible to get out of language, as modern philosophy seems to show us, and has done since Wittgenstein, action will necessarily become a utterance in order to be thought. Moreover, the statement itself, and even more specifically the legal statement, implies an essential part of performativity. In this sense, if "to do" is always to say, then it can be "a doing."[9] It is in this perspective that the discovery of the performative dimension of language and its relevance to the understanding of legal discourse, is placed. These two dimensions[10] are usually distinct in legal analysis.

A distinction is thus made between the values placed on legal statements and their validity. Reference to a value provides a measure of an object by reference to an external element (e.g., language), whereas validity reflects, more specifically, the good health of that object. Thus, three approaches to the validity of deontological statements can be identified, deontology being characterised by a reflection on what is duty as a modality and on what can be the value and interest of logic for the benefit of the deontology.[11] The legal statement can be apprehended from an examination of its syntactic, pragmatic or semantic validity. In these various situations, validity is the predicate either of an act that has deontic status (deontic states of affairs) or of an act that has deontic status (deontic states of affairs). It is pragmatic validity, or deontic states of affairs posed by performative deontic acts (it is syntactic validity); or the validity of deontic utterances. It is semantic validity,

8 P. AMSELEK, "Le locutoire et l'illocutoire dans les énonciations relatives aux normes juridiques," in *Ecrits de philosophie du droit*, Panthéon-Assas, Paris, pp. 441–446.

9 This is what the work on performativity has shown us since at least Austin and Benveniste to refer only to the modern period.

10 We use this topological approach because the relationship between utterance and enunciation expresses two information spaces that we believe are heterogeneous. The saying and the saying that I say form fields of information that are generally apprehended as different because they are apprehended from the question of meaning and the meaning or *a contrario* of the action. It is only in performative approaches to language that we manage to sew these two fields of information together, but with a loss of information.

11 The very important philosopher and jurist G.A. Conte distinguishes on this theme three questions: a *noétique question* (which deals with the presence of a possible truth which would be specific to the deontic), *dianetic* (the analysis of logical relations between norms) *dianomic (the* analysis of the relations between the validity of one deontic entity and the validity of another deontic entity).

which then imposes the question of the reference of the utterance and finally brings the question inherent in semantic validity closer to the – classical – question of truth in the philosophical sense. These three approaches can be apprehended from two situations that the philosophy of normative language has developed since the work of Professor A. Tale from the aspects of theticity and athetics; for example, for syntactic validity, which is the most common for the jurist, theticity is analyzed as the fact that the validity of a deontic entity (a norm) is the product of whether it is posed by a deontic act.

In this perspective an enunciation generates deontic acts whose pragmatic validity can be appreciated under a thetical and an athetical aspect. Moreover, this act produces in a specific way a deontic entity whose validity can also be assessed thetically and athetically by the study of syntactic validity. Finally, this entity will be able to establish a particular relation to the world which can be apprehended from the study of its semantic validity.

In this sense, a legal statement has the value of a speech act and is valid with respect to various dimensions of the speech act.[12]

The concept of validity for the lawyer leads him or her to value one dimension of the validity of the speech act that forms the legal statement, to the detriment of the complexity of the latter. In this sense, the syntactic, i.e., legal validity in the classical sense of the term, and semantic dimensions of the validity of a legal statement thus shield the pragmatic validity of the statement.

The pragmatic validity of the legal statement expresses the idea of the "good health" of the act of speech from the specific way it acts *on* or *in the* world. Indeed, it is when the act of language generates a "state of affairs" and causes an alteration of the world;[13] conversely, when the act of language no longer imposes itself on the world, but takes place in the world, we generally speak of the inclusion of a practice in the world.[14]

With regard to what was previously stated when the Constitutional Court in the decision in question noted that "in view of the particular circumstances of the case, there is no reason for judging that this organic law was adopted in violation of the procedural rules provided for in Article 46 of the Constitution," it therefore gives rise to a specific performativity.

Our thesis as presented above is that the particularism of the decision results from the disappearance of the screen between the statement and the enunciation. It will therefore be necessary to specifically analyze the pragmatic validity of the performative act. The performative act generates a deontic state of affairs, starting with an act of creation that must be specified in order to study its specific validity. The pragmatic validity of the act in question (the enunciation of the constitutional judge) is presented either as a *praxis* or as a *poiesis*. It thus expresses two different ways of acting *in* and *on the* world. It is a matter of either changing the world by the making of a thing or of an action that generates a *praxis* that is done in the

12 On this distinction see P. AMSELEK, *Cheminements philosophiques dans le monde du droit et des règles en général*, Armand Colin, Paris, 2012, p. 180.

13 It is then similar to older languages presented as *factio* or *poiesis*.

14 We're talking about *präxis* or *actio*.

world. As such, the decision of the constitutional judge seems more a *praxis* than a *poiesis*.[15] It notes a reality more than it proclaims the existence of a deontic entity.

Concretely, the decision of the constitutional court as an enunciation act is theologically valid either praxonomically or praxistically. In accordance with this analysis, the validity of the act of enunciation must therefore be examined either with regard to the concept (praxeological) that it implements (it is a decision), or with regard to the necessary conditions[16] linked to the validity of the enunciation and which are imposed by the legal order. In the present case, in particular, Article 61 of the Constitution and Order No. 58–1067 of November 7, 1958 on the Organic Law on the Constitutional Council as amended by Order No. 59–223 of February 4, 1959Y and by Organic Laws No. 74–1101 of December 26, 1974 and No. 90–383 of May 10, 1990, No. 95–63 of January 19, 1995, No. 2007–223 of February 21, 2007, No. 2008–695 of July 15, 2008, No. 2009–403 of April 15, 2009, No. 2009–1523 of December 10, 2009, No. 2010–830 of July 22, 2010, No. 2011–333 of March 29, 2011, No. 2011–410 of April 14, 2011, No. 2013–906 of October 11, 2013, No. 2013–1114 of December 6, 2013.

Beyond the validity of the pragmatic enunciation and now concerning the result of this enunciation, the deontic state of affairs is syntactically valid either on a thetical or on an athetical basis. In the present case, the idea that the validity of the state of affairs engendered can be valid on the basis of the respect of a norm that can found it in, and through the ordering is delicate, because precisely this decision seems to violate the Constitution in a formal way. Validity would therefore be atheistic. It merely "codifies" a status and does not proclaim a status. The statement is therefore declarative, not proclamatory.

It is at this level that the singularity of this decision is shown and to understand the situation, it is appropriate to refer to the analysis made by Th. Geiger[17] who studied the philosophy of normative language by G.A. Conte. In his work on the sociology of law, Geiger distinguishes three paradigms that make it possible to clarify the functioning of law. He distinguishes the presence of deontic regularity and adéontic regularity (which could be rendered as rules and regularities); he also

15 Pragmatic validity is that which, starting from the enunciation itself, makes it possible to relate the enunciation either to a constitutive rule which necessarily lays down the conditions for pragmatic validity (we speak of praxeonomic validity); or, if it is impossible to relate the enunciation to such a rule, to perceive an athetical and praxeological pragmatic validity (such as a promise, for example) which is valid as an act of enunciation, because it is in conformity with its concept. It should be noted that in the case of praxeonomic validity, the rule poses a necessary condition; it is thus a subset of the anankastico-constitutive rules. It poses the necessary condition of what it is the rule of which it is the rule. On these questions the work of Conte and the thesis of G.M. AZZONI, *Condizioni costitutive*, 1986.

16 For the decision of the constitutional court to exist, necessary but not sufficient conditions must be met.

17 Th. GEIGER, *Vorstudien zu einer Soziologie des Rechts*, Munksgaard, Copenhagen, 1947. For a synthetic reflection on these analyses: A.G. CONTE, "Nomotropismo: agire in funzione di regole," in *Filosofia del linguaggio normativo*, III, Giappichelli, Torino, 2001, pp. 895–920.

distinguishes norms from deontic utterances; and, finally, he distinguishes "declarative" deontic utterances and "proclamatory" deontic utterances. The declarative deontic statement expresses the observation that a norm subsists without it being able to be posed beforehand; i.e., without it being posed theoretically, which suggests the possibility of norms without statements by a statement. This is clearly what is happening in the case before us, in which the constitutional judge is thus content to note or codify a norm that *subsists* in the *reality of* a society: things being what they are, the judge could not do otherwise in the facts of the case, and it is ultimately on this pragmatic basis that the judge's decision is based. The syntactic validity of the statement, i.e., validity in the classical sense of the law, thus paradoxically results from its conformity to an athetical validity. This athetical validity is based on a semantic relationship to the world suggesting that in the deontic state of things there is a deontic reality that is not constituted, but preconstituted; i.e., already there, subsisting and which must simply be codified.

The Constitutional Court's decision shows that under certain conditions of limited and extreme enunciations the enunciation and the enunciation on a point that normally remains invisible, is in the form of a principle in the sense of balancing of interests. In these exceptional situations, this borderline point of a discourse is the one which, by a twisting effect, is then presented as the ordinary point of a decision and expresses its tragic dimension.[18] Regularity replaces the rule, atheistic pragmatic validity underpins the syntactic validity of a statement,[19] and this at the price of transgressing our ordinary conception of legal validity.

To better understand it, we will now try to show this topology of transgression[20] that seems to us to be present in the decision of the constitutional judge, and we will analyze this question according to two approaches.

II The monstration: The space of the performative paradox

A The construction of the judge's argumentative space

When the judge thus makes a break, he expresses the idea of an evolution in the judge's line of argument and an inflection towards another line of argument. In positive law, the legal norm is therefore by its very nature – as an object subject to the

18 What is presented as tragic is the feeling of a certain loss of the world.... This notion is present in some form in the analysis of the scepticism inherent in the philosophy of ordinary language as we shall see.

19 In a similar logic, normativist and institutionalist approaches are complementary and compatible. They are compatible, because they answer different questions: the institution applies to the necessary and sufficient conditions of the legal order and normativism answers the questions *quid ius*? and *quid iuris*? they are complementary, because it is by means of norms that the system of institutionalisation etc. is based. On this question A.G. CONTE, "Cronotopo deontico," in *Filosofia del linguaggio normativo* III, Giappichelli, Torino, 2001, pp. 751–772.

20 D. MARRANI, "Transgression as the big bang of the society," in *Space, Time, Justice*, Routledge, London, 2018, pp. 1–16. D. CREWE, "Socio-Cultural Origins of Law," in *Transgression and Deviance*, Palgrave Macmillan, UK, 2013.

will of the person who by this means measures what it is possible for him to do[21] – always led to be duplicated. This question has been approached in legal theory in the classic form of the *Oreste*[22] paradox and has been studied by A. Conte in a famous article.[23] It is thus always possible to take two antagonistic directions from the rule (as it is possible to follow a straight line from two infinites).

Between two interpretations, between two texts, between a text and an enunciation, the projection of law in the world is at stake. In this sense, we can illustrate our argument in the form of a line that is placed on a space. This space would have as its dimensions those that are specific to legal discourse and, more broadly, to language itself, i.e., syntax and semantics. To remain coherent and not to contradict each other, the judge – or the legal operators – develop an argument that, like a line, will never cross a contrary argument; it will be conducted in parallel with the latter.

21 On this conception of the ruler as a measure of what is possible: cf., of course, the work of Professor Amselek. *Cf.* P. AMSELEK, *Écrits de philosophie du droit,* Panthéon-Assas, Paris, 2019. "[T]he rules appear to be in the field of metrology: their general function is to serve as a measure.... More precisely, they are reference tools, witness tools, giving the measure of the possible" (*op. cit.* p. 18).

22 The Orestes of Aeschylus (in Greek Ὀρέστεια) is composed of a cycle of three tragedies: *Agamemnon, The Choephorians, The Eumenides.* It is probably one of the greatest poetic works of antiquity. It is interesting to observe that these three pieces form a system and appear to be dialectically linked. *Agamemnon* thus forms the preamble to the general work. The initial theme of this tragedy is the murder of the King of the Greeks, on his return from the Trojan War, by his wife *Clytemnestra and* his accomplice and lover *Egisthe.* The intervention of the divine will, marked by Cassandra's prophetic revelations, gives a horrible domestic murder a fatal and sacred character and thus hints at the true significance of the work. The *Choephores* stage the punishment of the first crime (marital murder) by a second (a crime committed against his own blood): *Orestes* son of *Agamemnon* will thus kill his mother. With the help of his sister *Electra,* he will thus avenge the death of his father by the death of the two culprits. Thereafter he will seek refuge in Delphi, in the temple of the god who led his hand and who formally led him by the voice of his oracle to avenge the crime: *Apollo.* The *Eumenides,* finally, mark the reconciliation of *Orestes* with the Gods. Pursued by the *Furies* (the *Erinyes*) who punish the matricides (they are furious and consider that Orestes' crime is of a very different nature from the one he is supposed to have avenged: thus opposing a "marital crime" and a "crime of blood"). For the latter, the blood shed by *Clytemnestra,* unlike that of Orestes, is not that of his own race. From then on, *Orestes* is driven out of Delphi by *Pythia* and hides in Athens at the feet of the statue of *Athena.* Athena then proposed to establish a tribunal (the Athenian Aeropagus) and indicated that in the event of a parity of votes, she herself would tip the balance by taking a stand: she thus voted in favour of Orestes (in this vote the operation was specifically carried out by an act involving the laying of a "stone" which tipped the trial to one side: ψῆφος). This goddess, by her eloquence, thus calms the *Furies,* who then take on a new name, the *Eumenides* ("benevolent") and blesses the soil of Attica, where a sanctuary will be dedicated to them in the midst of public celebrations and festivities. This text is generally regarded by jurists as the one that envisages, for the first time, the possibility of a trial in which the judgment is handed down by a popular jury: the passage from revenge to justice in a way. It is thus likely to engender a perception of justice understood as the golden means - the point of balance - on which actors agree within an argumentative space. That will not be our angle and what we will be dealing with.

23 This question is discussed by A.G. CONTE, in the text: *Codici deontici,* 1976.

Traditionally, legal argumentation is motivated and developed to attract the conviction of an audience and not to appear as a mere act of authority. The argumentative space that thus emerges from the two arguments (for and against a thesis) thus cuts an argumentative structure in the space of two-dimensional legal discourse (syntactic and semantic). The paradox of this activity is that if the discussion goes on strangely long enough, the arguments are reversed and it often happens that the opposite of what was initially proposed is stated. We have all experienced this inversion and it is enough for the argument to last long enough to know this inversion. The initial determinism of a discourse is thus not able to calculate the totality of the influences of the context on what will be argued over time. This means that, in the end, the discourses are reversed and the edges of the argumentative band cross each other.

This argumentative duality that the rule finally expresses and its transgression can be brought back to the unity of a regularity as a straight line pushed to infinity is only a loop. What I know about the rule is corrected by what I do with the rule, and vice versa. The decision that is important to us is more strongly visible because the judge literally does not discuss it. The French Constitutional Court's decision violates this rule in the sense of its syntactic validity, and this for the benefit of recognizing a regularity. The transgression applies only to the rule, whereas regularity could only be recognised on the basis of the singularity of the subject's enunciation.

The performative paradox then takes the following form: one must do what I say and not what I do. The problem lies in the fact that when it is pushed to its limit, as in the present case, the paradox, which bases the syntactic validity of an utterance without showing it, on a pragmatic validity of the utterance, which could be athetical, *shows* itself and offers to observe that legal reason is posed retroactively only as the cause of what it explains: regularity is the object of immersion in a rule.

B The contribution of projective geometry: The paradox

This situation can be perfectly illustrated by the so-called projective geometry.[24] Naturally, in our hypothesis, it is only a question of imaginary grasping what is of the order of pure abstraction and this through the intermediation of a *monstrative*

24 Let's start with a brief reminder of what a projective plan is. This notion is present within the projective geometry theorised by Girard Desargues. The purpose of this notion is to allow us to analyse transformations in a freer way than in the case of Euclidean or affine geometry. In Erlangen's program presented in Felix Klein, a hierarchy of geometries is proposed that makes projective geometry the mother geometry. The various geometries would thus be particular cases of projective geometry, which encompasses them all. The latter offers to no longer have to distinguish cases and to demonstrate very general results. This projective geometry also apprehends infinity as a point on the plane. It is this aspect that will be essential for us. In projective geometry the parallel lines intersect in a point of the plane. All parallel lines intersect at infinity. More precisely they intersect twice at the beginning and at the end of the two lines (in both directions of the lines). By doing so we change our conception of straight lines and curves: in projective geometry, if we move along a straight line to infinity to the point of infinity we find ourselves on the other side of the line: paradoxically we can go around a straight line which then has the same shape as a circle.

geometry. It is a question of showing what our thought perceives in order to offer tracks to apprehend a reality constructed by the artifices of an articulation, inherent in our language, between law and facts. The reference to geometry offers to show the grammar of a practice, and therefore its proper use. For the presentation of these ideas see the illustration in the appendix at the end of this text.

In the present case, it is a question of grasping in this *imaginary* way the form of a practice which involves including facts in the law, starting with the facts of language. To show how, in the act of establishing the law, there are negotiated caesuras between the deontic and the addeontic (the notic caesura, the dianoetic caesura and the axiological caesura).[25]

This caesura implies that it is logically impossible to infer in legal discourse the relationship between facts and law.[26] However, there is "something" in the legal practice of legal operators that tames this limit and that the law is logically incapable of stating in its own discourse. Our proposal will then be to show it; that is, to show this fact of obviousness which is strangely always hidden and which implies that the ultimate truth of an enunciation lies in what the one who enunciates has done: the truth is that he has said it.[27]

We find here the idea of a change of intellectual tool similar to the one that for certain transformations makes projective geometry prevail over Euclidean geometry. The former offers the possibility of a thought inherent in this difference between what "I know" and what "I see." In the legal field, what "I know" if I am positivist, is that the validity of a legal norm can only be deduced from its relation to positive law, and that the law is in itself its own norm. In this sense, I accept this dogmatic "fact" in order to better integrate that in reality I know nothing about the law itself. This is the fascinating mystery of the tautology on which positive law itself is based. But I see this mystery *in the implementation of* law. In an immanent way, the latter makes me see its limit. In a way, it is a question of making visible an impossible object: the very object of the chiasmus between law and fact.[28]

25 According to Professor Conte between law and fact (between the deontic and the non deontic) there are three caesura which prevent logical inferences: a caesura between concepts (noétique), statements (dianétique) or truths (axiological). Cf. *Minima deontica, op. cit.*, p. 398.

26 This is the nature of Hume's famous paradox. On this question *see*, J.-L. GARDIES,*L'erreur de Hume*, PUF, Paris, 1987.

27 It is the pragmatic validity of the utterance that is at stake. Here we find an approach to truth as developed by Quine on the basis of Tarski's work and his famous T convention. For Quine, unlike for example Popper, Tarski's analysis does not refer to a corresponding truth. For the American philosopher, correspondence is not between the terms of a theory and reality, but a correspondence between two theories. Saying of an assertion that it is true is simply to reaffirm it. What is true is the statement, but its truth consists in the fact that it exists in the world as the statement says. W.V. QUINE, *La poursuite de la vérité*, Seuil, Paris, 1993.

28 It is, in a way, to think of "immersing" or "plunging" one plane into another. To allow the subject of the utterance to be immersed or immersed in the space inherent in the subject of the utterance. Immersion means a transformation of an object by

Thus, in projective geometry and in the constitution of a "projective plane" what was parallel will tend to infinity in a vanishing point that is paradoxically included in the plane. All parallel lines have a vanishing point and all vanishing points can be found on a line that intersects all the infinites that can be deduced from the various parallel lines: a straight line that intersects the horizon of the various projective lines.

What thus makes the interest of a projective plan is this line which frames the Euclidean space and passes through all the vanishing points: it is the limit of the projective plan, its reason. It should be added that like a two-directional line, the vanishing point is located at the two extremities of the line. In this sense, the line that passes through all the infinite points is in fact a circle. We can easily understand this by using the figure of a sphere to see that the straight lines that appear on it as meridians converge towards the two poles but are locally parallel. Lines having two directions in projective geometry are reduced to a single point and the line will take the form of a loop. The projective lines are homeomorphic to a circle. They are in the form of a closed straight line with a point at infinity. In the same way in the legal field, divergent arguments are found at the limit in this boundary or this "horizon of reasonableness" which delimits the argumentative space of the law: it is then enough to argue long enough.

In addition, this projector line offers another special feature. As the projective lines take the form of a loop, it is possible to move in a certain way from one infinity to the other and thus continuously along this loop. In a Euclidean shot, one would naturally have the impression of appearing on one side of the shot and then the other and thus in the manner of the character of the game who disappears at the edge of the screen and reappears on the other side. In law, the oppositions are balanced by principles that reconcile the opposites and express the reason for the argumentative lines at the limit. This seems to explain the practical success of proportionality, balancing of interests, *ragionevolezza,* etc. These notions allow to calm the shocks in the inversions between spaces with different dimensions and to facilitate the immersions and dives.

In the above example, the two sides that are glued together belong to a two-dimensional object (the reconciliation of two arguments that belong to the same order). The situation is different when we consider sewing together more complex and heterogeneous objects such as spaces, as is the case, for example, between law and fact, statement and enunciation, and doing and saying.

The projective plane is un-representable in a two-dimensional space. Indeed, it is easy to understand that the limit of the projective plane, which is composed of the various points at infinity, implies being able to represent, for each point, an infinite number of circles that pass through this point. The projective plane is thus what is presented as a surface without an edge and understood as non-directable, because it is unilateral, it has only one side like the famous Moebius strip. The reality of this topology never consists of two sides: one outside and one inside. As

introducing it into a different environment. If the final object is entirely equivalent to the original object, it is called immersion, otherwise it is called immersion.

a certain realism in philosophy demonstrates, the thought of reality is not a way of accessing it from some interiority, but a way of making it from it, of norming it from it. In this sense, reality is what it *is* and imposes *its* norm (this is what we believe A.G. Conte did with its paradox and its difference between rule and regularity). When we move from the "political real" to the "legal real," it is not possible to dive in, but only to immerse oneself in order to represent it.

Naturally, this comes at a price. To be rendered by immersion, the surface that joins non-homogeneous spaces will self-intersect. To be able to stick together, the two spaces will sew their edges together by crossing and cutting the straight lines[29] and fictitiously express an inversion of the object (for us an inversion of the object of the discourse of law). Where saying and doing express a unique reality, that of an act of speech, in the narrower dimension of the legal statement, we will perceive an opposition between the two. This opposition will be all the stronger the shorter the argument, as in the decision that is important to us.

The passage through projective geometry thus metaphorically offers the possibility[30] of perceiving that the enunciation is immersed in the utterance and that this place of the enunciation is never given back "as a whole" in the law. Moreover, this immersion of the enunciation in the order of law implies an inversion; some would say a reversal.[31]

The thing then appears as what is symmetrically the opposite. It is in the positive statement of the legal operator in times of crisis that chiasmus is thus *shown*. It comes in various potential forms. With this figure, what manifests itself is the part of transgressive power inherent in the legal enunciation that appears by breaking into the meaning of the text.[32] Professor Timsit called this "breaking of meaning."[33] The literal transcription is then overwhelmed by the "transcription" or "transgression."[34] Another form is possible from the distinction between

29 For a demonstration: analysis-situs.math.cnrs.fr/Quelques-surfaces-non-orientables. Html. The projective plane RP2 is the set of straight lines of R3 passing through the origin. As each of these lines intersects the sphere: S2={(x,y,z)∈R3 | x2+y2+z2=1}. At two points symmetrical with respect to the origin, the projective plane can be seen as the quotient of S2 by the involution: (x,y,z)→(-x,-y,-z).(x,y,z)→(-x,-y,-z).As this involution reverses the orientation of the sphere, the projective plane is not orientable. This is the first example of a closed non-orientatable surface. The link offers a video representation of this type of immersion.

30 On this question of metaphor: E. BORDES, *Le silence et le droit, recherches sur une métaphore,* PUL, Quebec, 2018; G. TIMSIT, "La métaphore dans le discours juridique," *Revue européenne des sciences sociales,* 38 (117), (2000), pp. 83–94; G. LAKOFF and M. JOHNSON, *Les métaphores dans la vie quotidienne*, Editions de minuit, Paris, 1985.

31 This idea of a reversal is present, for example, in Merleau-Ponty's thinking and in the implementation of his concept of flesh. For him the fold is thus a winding and twisting. "Flesh … is not contingency, chaos, but a texture that returns in itself and suits itself": M. MERLEAU-PONTY, *Le visible et l'invisible,* Gallimard, Paris, 1964, p. 190.

32 A distinction must be made between the meaning and the meaning of the text. Classically, meaning is oriented by denotation to a reality, whereas meaning is involved in a connotative relationship.

33 G. TIMSIT, "Sur deux points aveugles de la doctrine juridique: nouvelles considérations sur le dialogisme normatif", in *Mélanges André Lajoie,* pp. 359–379.

34 On this question: *La transgression*, Bruylant, Bruxelles, 2013.

compatibility and conformity drawn by Ch. Eiseinmann, which offers legal operators the possibility of allowing certain illegal consequences to occur.[35] The vanishing point from which this inversion takes place may consist, for example, in the social effectiveness of the law in its realism.[36]

In the recent decision of the Constitutional Court, this situation is once again taking shape. The members of the Constitutional Council cannot ignore the truth of what they say. Paradoxically, it is summed up in the fact that they are saying it. There is thus a certain courage to get involved in a transgression in the name of the effectiveness of what is said in the place where it is said. This shows a reflexivity effect of the judge on his function.

III Ethical justification of performativity: Assuming cynicism

It thus seems possible to trace the outlines of a certain ethic inherent in this position of the legal operator vis-à-vis his function. Indeed, if this consideration of the irrefutable part of the utterance in the statement is unavoidable, it testifies when it is *shown* at this point to a certain logic that questions the ethics of the speaker (A). For all that, however legitimate it may be in its ability to provoke an adult conversation about agreement *in* our democracy, it must remain a full act and not become a habit (B).

A The tragedy of *meaning: The assumed cynicism of the law*

The question of transgression offers by pushing the right to its limits to perceive the presence of a "mental concept"[37] that is usually transparent. If the law offers in its own register only the recognition of a situation and not the knowledge of it, it is appropriate to mourn the latter. The real transgression would therefore not be the possibility of moving to the other side, but simply the abandonment of that very possibility. The screen of law would be its limit and its internal censorship. This necessary acceptance of the abandonment or mourning of a mythical transgression is of the order of the tragic. The consideration of it by the judge is the only true ethical effort, because it imposes to reintegrate the relationship to the other, no longer in the form of a discourse *on the* world, but in that of a fragile agreement *in the* world as expressed in the discourse that offers the recognition of it.

This ethical action, the outlines of which could be traced, then takes the form of a reflection on the tragedy and its turnarounds. Studies on this literary genre – or on this form of expressivity – are useful to grasp the substance of this form, which is attached to what in philosophy is treated as the question of skepticism. The

35 Ch. EISENMANN, "Le droit administratif et le principe de légalité," *EDCE*, 1957, pp. 25–40.

36 On this question, see the remarkable analysis of M. REVERT, "Le droit administratif français et la transgression," in *La transgression*, Bruylant, Bruxelles, 2013, pp. 261–282.

37 It is perhaps the presence of this myth perfectly apprehended by J. Bouveresse, which has to do with interiority: the thought of "wanting to say" does not take place in our heads.

meaning of tragedy thus derives from the refusal to recognise something that relates to oneself. Usually what is so tragic is the refusal to perceive or publicly accept what is of oneself in what is stated. This is, of course, even more strongly challenged when the statement is elaborated as the word of the Other. The judge thus says "the law, the law …" by attaching himself to a meaning that is "already there" and that results from an act of intelligence; the judge endeavors to conceal the reality of the act of creation and the place of his will in implementing the meaning.

The tragedy therefore lies in the belief that access to legal knowledge, by its very nature, always fails, and in the apparent foreclosure of the law as a tool. In the ordinary tragedy, litigation offers judges the opportunity to recover doubt through the claims of others.[38] The "legal knowledge" or the action of "legal qualification" are always brought to a certain limit by the claims. The tragic question put to the judge is whether he *really* wants to know is the basis of the decision and, above all, how to *recognise it*. This is what we will present as a tragedy of meaning, which too rarely implies a perfectly assumed cynicism.

Tragedy expresses a specific emotion that is formulated in terms of the correlation that naturally arises between the world and man. There is no doubt that we are currently facing a tragedy and that the decision of the constitutional judge is taken in this specific context of enunciation. There is, in the nature of the tragic perspective, the necessary taking into account of a certain refusal that must be questioned. This is inherent in the will that men seem to cling to – and which tragedy as a literary genre manifests – in the recognition of "something" that is of the order of failure.

In the decision of the constitutional judge, this failure seems to be perfectly conscious. It is even reinforced by the absence of any real justification and by the lapidary manner in which the writing is turned. Admittedly, the reference to the "particular circumstances of the case" testifies to the fact that it is the situation of enunciation which justifies the decision, but the demonstration remains brutally concise. Normally, it is this part of cynicism which is obscured and disappears under the flow of the legal enunciation of its justification in law and the movement of legal inferences. We recognise the judge's pragmatism and certainly the influence within the Constitutional Council of the members of the Conseil d'État, but there is something tragic about this in the sense that a certain philosophy understands it.

What the tragic dimension manifests, for example, when it is apprehended in the work of S. Cavell, is the impossibility of finding oneself "as a whole" as the subject of the enunciation in any statement and the great difficulty of appearing even a little bit in it. It is the presence of the "body" of judges, by appearing too much as the source of the enunciation, that is monstrous. Cavell analyzes in his work the question of tragedy by evoking the fact that what is attractive in this literary form is the question it raises about our capacity to really recognise ourselves as pretensions (as voices) in tragic stories.

38 S. CAVELL, *Dire et vouloir dire*, Cerf, Paris, 2009: "Tragedy is the place where one cannot escape the consequences of this overlapping of one issue by the other," p. 33

In the decision that matters to us, the voice of the constitutional judge is thus heard *in* our "life form." What the judge is transgressing is the idea that the law might know about the events overhanging it. It is the idea that the law could be in tune with the reality on which it is based and that the judge has total control over it.

In a tragedy, what we usually discover is the following:

> What shows up is that the reason why the consequences are stalking us so furiously is not simply that we are half-blind and unlucky, but that we persevere in doing the thing that produced those consequences in the first place. What we need is not rebirth, or being saved, but courage, or simple prudence, to see and stop. To surrender.[39]

In this decision the constitutional judge abdicated a certain mythological perception of the Constitution and the rule of law. He expresses that he cannot but take note of the fact that in the situation in which he finds himself and at the time when he has to decide he can only do what he does. There is an abdication of "meaning" in favor of "use."

From this perspective, the decision of the constitutional judge cannot be moral, but it does seem to me to be perfectly ethical. Indeed, this decision does not comply with the imperative of the norm in the Kantian sense, but with the awareness of a certain regularity. Here we find the opposition between rules and regularities mentioned above, as well as the emergence of a conceptual category that is neglected in law (the concepts of disposition). When the judge summons the rule, he imposes a moral duty on himself, and this duty is collective: morality is always in some way the morality of the Other. When the judge calls for regularity, he or she is attaching to an ethic. He will have to find *his* voice (his way) in the tragic relationship that will be established with regard to the claims of others. He will have to engage his responsibility and thus answer personally for the decision as an expression of a will: the king is naked.

In this ethical act, the legal operator is fully inscribed in the whirlwind of a life form and not overhanging it. This ethical manifestation is finally quite rare in the legal and political field: responsible ethics easily deteriorates into irresponsible social morality, because it is shared in the manner of a deferred and misplaced belief. Reflections on the tragedy seem to show, moreover, that these ethical

39 S. CAVELL, *op. cit.* at 465. It should be noted that ethical behaviour manifests itself in the acceptance or rejection of a certain relationship to the world. In this sense, it explains both tragedy as rupture or doubt with regard to the world and comedy as reconciliation with regard to the world. This is what is at stake in remarriage comedies, which clearly pose the question of reconstructing a certain conversation. On this question: S. CAVELL, *À la recherche du bonheur: Hollywood et la comédie de remariage*, Cahiers du cinéma, Paris, 1993. On the relationship between law and cinema: "The collapse of the law of the father in the cinema of Refn. Featherstone, M. Primal Crime: Visions of the Law and Its Transgression in Nicolas Winding Refn's Cinema," *Int J Semiot Law* (2019). J.K. GWYNNE, *Anglo-American Cinema: Gender, Sex, and the Deviant Body*, Columbia University Press, New York, 2016, esp. pp.1, 31 & 80.

behaviors – which sometimes offend morality – are probably the only ones that can durably save morality itself.

In this sense, the hard ground of the rule – and this is what is expressed with the question "what is following a rule?" is the very existence of regularity. It is in the "conversation of justice" that the form of life which seems inherent in our democracy is woven. In order for it to really exist, it is necessary for everyone to speak in this way with his or her own voice. The position of the Constitutional Council is therefore ethical. It will naturally and necessarily be criticised and commented on for what it is: a position taken in the whirlwind of a form of life. What is perceived by some as a crisis of the rule of law and its morals would be nothing more than a refusal or a challenge to its metaphysics in favor of pragmatic validity. There is in the Council's decision a refusal of easy conviviality agreeing on a mythology and a way of testing the limits of our democracy in this way. Criticism and commentary will, in this way, have the force of a real conversation about what matters to us.

There is a space for rediscovering the important and not the fundamental. Then it will no longer be a matter of basing our agreement on a backward world, but in it. This emphasis on the important has been perfectly illustrated, in our opinion, by Cavell in his analysis of cinema. Cinematic discourse offers to perceive – by its very nature – an essential phenomenon with regard to the act of enunciation:

> The reading of a film triggers a permanent call to our experience of film.... It is true that once transcribed on paper, the words of a dialogue seem too poor to contain the meaning I want to put into it ... they must be removed from the paper and put back, in memory, on the screen.[40]

Everyone will have to face this decision by experimenting with the control of their experience. Without this confidence in our experience, which is expressed in the willingness to find words to say it, we are devoid of authority in our own experience. Without this trust our approach is moral, but it is not ethical.

This analysis of the tragedy implies that the truth of this decision results in the real acceptance of the following situation: we can neither get out of the language nor deny our responsibilities in it. And the responsibility of a discourse such as that of the jurist, in the end, is to offer certainties and the impression that we can effectively act on the world from it.[41] This is what Cavell expresses, in his own way, the difficulty of making his voice heard and speaking on behalf of the other.

40 S. CAVELL, *à LA recherche du bonheur: Hollywood et la comédie de remariage,* Cahiers du cinéma, Paris, 1993, p. 18.

41 As a specialist language implemented in ordinary language, the lawyer's discourse takes the form of a declination of the master's discourse as it is presented, for example, in the perspective offered by the Lacanian logic of discourse. We know that this discourse is the first and, as such, it is the one from which the other discourses are reflected upon. It has a specific structure that makes four logical places (truth, agent, work and product) occupy four instances: $\$\rightarrow S1\rightarrow S2–(a)$. These four instances are respectively. $ (the crossed-out subject: the one that comes about as a result of integration in language and which in a certain way is spoken); S1: the master signifier, that is to say the specific sign referring to the ideology; S2

B The virtue of an act and the risk of the farce

This ethical phenomenon had been perfectly clear by Schelling: it is an act by which I choose myself in language. As the German philosopher shows, there is thus an opposition if not an incompatibility between conscience and freedom. In the tragic play *Orestie*, cited above, Athena's free act seems paradoxically to obey an "inexorable necessity."[42] There is in the analysis of the decision an aspect that should therefore be clarified. The decision is free and sovereign, that is to say, indeterminate. The full and true decisive act is unconscious.[43] As expressed by a certain reading of Kant in conjunction with Wittgenstein, the mind is not so much confined to understand (which would imply *the* presence of a transcendental exterior) as confined to language. What the individual "freely" enunciates through an act of enunciation retroactively sets out the reasons for the act.

It is in this gap that the virtue of the act lies. It is understandable that, in this conception of the act, there are few true acts. Usually, they cause events and scandals. What then arises is the appearance of the effects of the provisions proper to human freedom.[44]

the set of words what Lacan presents as the "treasure of signifiers"; (a) the "remainder" that necessarily exists as a result of the gap between the subject of the enunciation and the subject of the utterance. The discourse of the master is the very discourse of language (of its colonization of the world) – it is the first to appear. Its structure is a particular configuration between four places: truth, agent, work and product. 1. Truth is naturally incompatible with respect to knowledge. Truth is posed retroactively, because it is only an empty place: it is the hypothetical prerequisite. It is what will, when reflexively questioned, cleanse the discourse of false certainties. It is a questioning of its own foundation for the benefit of the way in which a discourse develops. In this sense, when it is enunciated it cannot be the whole truth and is then deduced from the error. 2. The agent: he is the sensible materiality of the sign (the signifier not what is signified or the meaning that will be attributed to it). He is the semblant (S1 in Lacan's language): he is what stops the flow of signifiers and anchors it retroactively: the meaning of the signification for language. It is something that makes a sign to the being, but which does not yet have a meaning. The master assimilates himself *as* this master signifier. Paradoxically, it should be noted that the master is therefore in a certain way stupid, because he is by nature blind to the truth on which he is based: he works and makes work (we find this idea in functionalist and systemic analyses: for example, in Luhmann's work). 3. The other (knowledge, work): in the master's discourse what is assigned to this place is S2. It expresses a certain jouissance, each phenomenon is duplicated because of its existence in language and through language. The jouissance is thus a "drift" in language.

42 On this relationship between freedom and conscience in Schelling's work: S. ZIZEK, *Essai sur Schelling: le reste qui n'éclot jamais,* L'Harmattan, Paris, 2018, p. 22ff.

43 In the end, there is always initially always an act of self-determination: "the act by which one's life is determined in time does not itself belong to time, but to eternity: therefore it precedes life, not according to time, but through time (not grasped by it) as an eternal act according to nature. Through him, man's life extends to the beginning of creation; he is also outside what is created, free and itself an eternal beginning". F. W.J. SCHELLING, *Recherches sur la liberté humaine et les objets qui s'y rattachent,* Payot, Paris: 1977, p. 132.

44 In our opinion, this concept of virtue will be apprehended in a specific framework: that of dispositional realism developed for example by C. Tiercelin. This approach offers to think the causality apprehended according to an empirical approach. For the philosopher holding the chair of Metaphysics Philosophy of Science, it is a question of considering that dispositions are real and as such generate a causal dynamic. For a first

We can see how in law, the rules are set and are played out here, and this is done by an inversion that is counter-intuitive to the classical relationships that usually play between "being" and "becoming." In law, it is the sum of the uses that retroactively sets the rule as signifying. According to the same logic, the validity of a norm derives from its integration into a legal order. Validity plays in and through the legal order. The legal order itself is a question of fact and not of validity.

In this sense, a real decision or act always stalls a certain discourse and therefore expresses the necessary transgression of the transgression we have previously discussed. In fact, the decision reveals the space of a gap between two perceptions or two declinations of a situation. What hides this gap is the adherence (the internal point of view dear to jurists) to a certain ideology which is only the other name for belief. Perhaps the most powerful belief is the belief that it is possible to transgress it. In this sense, the lawyer sometimes gives in to the belief or ideology that the law can be transgressed in the name of justice, etc. The benefit of a reflexive transgression that transgresses in the name of the transgression itself offers the understanding that ultimately it is in the name of the enunciation's reality that this act takes place. Faced with this real deviation, there must always be the virtue (in the classical sense of force) of an act.

This stumbling block expresses our ability to fall in our relationship to life itself – to return to the hard ground of being and accept reality for what it is and only for what it is. What is scandalous is, in Badiou's expression, the manifestation from a corner of reality:

> The scandal is precisely what will … open the door to a kind of unveiling of a corner of reality, but at the price of this fragment being immediately treated as an exception.[45]

This ideological exception is not reality, only its semblance and only its theatricalization:[46] an expression of our reality. We have, therefore, contact with reality

approach to this question: C. TIERCELIN, *Le ciment des choses: petit traité de métaphysique scientifique réaliste, collection science et métaphysique*, Ithaque, Paris, 2011.

45 A. BADIOU, *A la recherche du réel perdu*, Fayard, Paris, 2015, p. 15. We can also imagine how the scandal apprehended in these terms can present itself as the bearer of the norm itself according to the adage that the exception is the basis of the rule. Cf. on these questions, the probative analysis of the exception that is developed in the work of G. AGAMBEN.

46 On this question the truculent analysis in Alain Badiou's Seminar (*Images du temps présent*: 2001–2004, Fayard, Paris) on Genet's play Le Balcon. It should be noted that this piece was written in 1956: however, it was commented on by Lacan in his seminar in March 1958. One recalls that it was during the month of May 1958 that the events in Algeria began with "Operation Resurrection". There is therefore a certain contemporaneity between these events which manifests a reality that will be interpreted by the psychoanalyst. According to the psychoanalyst, what this piece fully manifests is the desire of the Other. On March 13 Lacan deals with the Balcony and gives his definition of comedy: "comedy assumes, collects, enjoys the relation to an effect … namely the appearance of that signified which is called the phallus." In this sense, and in the register of the analysis of this appearance, comedy is thus apprehended (this is Badiou's thesis) as always a comedy of the present ("the stake of comedy is both to point out what in the present is power and to show that, as soon as it is shown, as soon as it appears, this power dissolves, makes

only through semblance: an exception that causes scandal and that offers us the possibility of falling back on the hard ground of being. The reality inherent in language is thus its internal limit.

All in all, what this decision tragically reveals is the revelation of a truth that is "skeptical" of a knowledge that is horrifying and monstrous. The law is an instrument and not the search for an adaptation to reality or a search for justice and happiness. Through the assumed cynicism of the judge, the reality of an ethical, if not moral, act is expressed which really shows from where the decision comes. Through this decision, the constitutional judge sets the conditions for a real conversation and offers the opportunity for adult learning of a democracy free of its ideological "backwardness."[47]

Naturally, and this is the infinitely risky gamble of such a decision, this tragic ethical effort has its own limits. In order not to become a caricature of what it is, this act that brings to its limits the justification of the legal statement must not become anything other than a free and exceptional act: under no circumstances can it become a habit. We are aware of the risk, in historical development, of a transformation of this kind and of the disappearance of the tragic in favor of what would be no more than a sad and painful farce.

Table 1.1 Synoptic tables of validities and relationships between the dimensions of validity

Deontic validity:	**Pragmatic** validity:	**Thetics**	**Athetics**
The performative act, the state of things conveyed by the statement and the relation to the world established on a semantic basis;	Validity of the act of theoretical normation A praxis (non-thetical) or a poiesis (thetical); Praxis can be rhetorical...	Manufacturing by deed is valid in *practice* The validity of the act is linked to the presence of a rule extrinsic to the act: for example, the rules which lay down in the various ordinances the conditions of necessary and constitutive validity	The manufacture by the act is valid *praxeologically the* validity of the act is assessed by its conformity to the concept.
		↓	↓
		Proclamations: following a rule	Consultative acts: codifying a regularity

(*Continued*)

spectacle of its nothingness, its emptiness", *op. cit.*, p. 19). What is the present represented by this comedy between 1956 and 1958? A brothel ...

47 On this question of learning to converse in a democracy, we refer to Cavell's analysis in the above-mentioned book *In Search of Happiness, op. cit.* and in particular in the chapter on words for a conversation: pp. 9–46.

Table 1.1 (Cont.)

		Syntactic validity: validity of the normative entity. Validity as generally understood by law.	**Thetics** Validity of a deontic status produced by a deontic act	**Athetics** Validity of a deontic status that is not produced by a deontic act
		Semantic validity: validity extended to a kind of truth and thus to a reference relationship	**Correspondence of the** statement to a deontic status	**Correspondence of** the norm to a deontic reality
Validity: The difference between deontic and logical validity is in metadeontics.	*Déontique* (Validity deontology)	Pragmatic: validity of deontic acts, validity is predicated on enunciation.	*Praxeological*: the enunciation is validated by the concept of the act itself. *Praxeonomic*: it relates to a hypothetical constitutive rule.	*Athetics*: e.g., the promise that conceptually is impossible for the past. *Theory*: the hypothetical constitutive rule sets the conditions for the validity of the act
		Syntax: status validity. This validity is predicated on status or deontic states of affairs (they are generally the product of deontic acts).	*Thetical*: this is validity in the classical sense of the term for a lawyer. It is apprehended by antonomasia. It is in and for a legal order and must be extended to the notico-constituent norm of the latter.*Athetics*: it seems to take the form of a paradox. It is not generated by a deontic act. It presents itself under two aspects: • In a *nomographic* form: there is codification in which a nomos is the **object of a description; it is, for** example, to describe a codified practice such as revenge in certain societies. • In a *nomothetic* form: there is a codification in which a nomos is the **subject of a position grant**. It is a matter of recognizing the presence of declarative statements (cf. this term). The statement is not the description of the act, but the act itself	

(*Continued*)

Table 1.1 (Cont.)

	Semantics: this is the validity of deontic statements. The difficulty in apprehending this notion results from the distinction between truth and validity. Validity is presented as the analogy of truth.	*Thetical*: it is the correspondence of the utterance to a deontic status or state of affairs constituted thematically by the deontic enunciation of the utterance itself. *Athetics*: it is the correspondence of the deontic utterance to a deontic status or a deontic state of affairs pre-constituted to the thetic enunciation of the deontic utterance itself.
	Logic: it is the examination of validity in the deontic field (deontic validity)	*Dianetics*: the validity of an inference is not an inference of validity (deontic validity). Discursive thinking mode. *Noétique*: intuitive way of thinking (noôs: mind, noésis: act of intelligence).

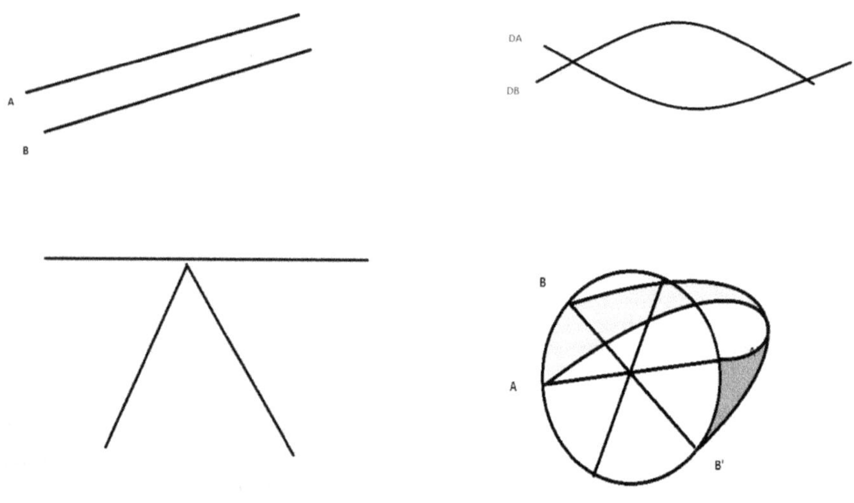

Figure 1.1 Topology and boundaries

Legend: Lines A and B show in a space the opposing arguments, which normally do not intersect except at the horizon, i.e., at the edge of the plane. These two straight lines intersect at the two horizons and thus form two circles. The latter corresponds to this logic and is understood from this projective point which is in this case the center of the circle. The band that makes up the space between the arguments A and B and A' and B' (the lines extend to infinity on both sides) are affected by a twist.

2 The category of "fundamental rights"

Fundamentality or the virtue of importance

This text seeks to reflect a renewed approach to "legal categories" which seems to us more necessary today than ever.[1] It is inferred from the integration of the contributions of the philosophy of ordinary language into legal thinking.[2] Nevertheless, this approach implies identifying an initial trap. Our reactions to the ordinary (and everyday) are generally of the order of "all for that!"

The conceptual apparatus that is mobilised to deal with the obvie and the ordinary – and therefore paradoxically with everything that is ordinarily important in life – is subject to denial and certainly to deep irritation: it would only be a question of "useless complexity"; "a discourse that could be avoided, because, in the end, things are what they are and the law is obviously always lagging behind its reality." Finally, it would be "the business of philosophers or sociologists and not the work of jurists." Naturally, the trap is reinforced by the fact that our judgement (which relates to this denial) is partly unfair and seems to lack nuance. In fact, there is in the legal field a certain perception of the ordinary and the obvious (the law is never totally disembodied: it is driven by human claims).

However, litigation, (which seems to us to be the main vehicle of law in relation to the ordinary, plays a paradoxical role: that of an "evanescent mediator."[3] He

1 Specifically it is at a time in our history when the fundamental and the important make a sudden burst into our daily life and when these legal categories are called upon to allow the continuation of the ordinary of our form of life.

2 That is to say, a grammar of everyday life that would be a re-remembering and re-appropriating the rules of language that have, in a way, been forgotten in practice and usage. There are thus principles of articulation which are inscribed in a specific practice and environment. In this respect, we would be our own *nomothetes* in ordinary language, unlike a specialty language or a foreign language. There is, in this sense, an "official grammar" which would be the very condition for forgetting the "ordinary grammar." This philosophy lays the emphasis on the ordinary because it is the ordinary that manifests and expresses what is important. This must be understood in the sense that the closest is ultimately the most important, while unfortunately, generally speaking, the ordinary is sent back into the distance for the benefit of a certain metaphysics. The risk of not taking this concept of the ordinary seriously is that it becomes a concept *about the* world.

3 F. JAMESON presents this notion in his analyses of Weber: "The Vanishing Mediator Narrative structure in Max Weber," *New German Critique* 1, pp. 52–82. He is both a screen and the screen on which things are projected.

DOI: 10.4324/9781003130109-3

acts as if the everyday nature of litigation generates, by its very movement, a denial of the ordinary or a recomposition of the ordinary. He then acts as a legal scaffolding, dedicated to reaching the ordinary of the situation through the legal qualification of the facts, which is juxtaposed to the ordinary. The law becomes immune to this question of the ordinary by affirming that it elaborates its own translation of the world. Being itself its own norm (positive law being, as such, what the law considers to be the law) its ontology is naturally stipulative. Consequently, the relationship to the world would thus be outside the law. As such, it would be impossible to derive a theory from a legal object through language, but only a theory of its meanings or uses.[4]

However, these analyses, however accurate they may be, do not seem to prevent us from developing a relevant epistemological reflection on our modalities of knowledge.

Legal thinking, which builds and elaborates, is second with regard to the world it inhabits and in which it develops. It cannot totally hide this fact. The question is, in this way, here as elsewhere: do we know what we mean when we say it?[5]

In the construction of legal categories, positive law thus functions as follows: it elaborates criteria on the basis of concepts that it gives as self-evident. The action of the legal operator is therefore to determine whether this or that thing is "the case" of this or that other thing. The positive norm which is used by the operator as the relevant criterion for his action is thus, for him, the measure of what is legally possible.

In legal practice, the concept (the conventional test) precedes the standard criteria implementation. By this very fact it is in a way dangerously naturalised (it is understood as an essence). In this analysis, we shall focus on the legal category of "fundamental rights," because it reveals (in the ordinary course of its practice and

4 Professor O's position is known. PFERSMANN'S position, as perfectly summarised in his "Sketch of a theory of fundamental rights" in which he states as follows: "even if one accepts a Wittgensteinian definition ... of the meaning that is now widely used in the philosophy of language, according to which it is nothing other than usage, the identification of the uses of 'fundamental' and 'fundamental right' does not make it possible to construct a theory of fundamental rights, but only a theory of the multiple meanings/uses of these expressions in multiple contexts. Indeed, a distinction must be made between the construction of a given object < F> and the analysis of the object < meanings/uses of the expression "fundamental rights" in multiple contexts >. In the first case, a single use is fixed by convention, in the second case, multiple regularities of multiple uses are identified. The analysis of the use of this term in various contexts makes it possible to grasp the range of meanings of this expression in everyday discourse, but does not make it possible to construct a theory of the object, because everyday language, even technical, does not have to be concerned with contradictions or shifts in meaning." *Droit des libertés fondamentales,* 1st ed., L. FAVOREU et al., eds, Dalloz, Paris, p. 96.

5 Cf. on this question: S. CAVELL, *Dire et vouloir dire,* Cerf, Paris, 2009. But also D. Dennett and his theory of consciousness. On this question, in particular, the distinction developed between reporting and expressing on the basis of D. Rosenthal's analyses. D. DENNETT, *La conscience expliquée,* O. Jacob, Paris: 1993. Specifically on this question pp. 378–385. D. ROSENTHAL, "Thinking that One Thinks," ZIF report, No. 11, Research Group on Mind and Brain, Perspectives in Theorical Psychology and the Philosophy of Mind, Zentrum für Interdisciplinäre Forschung, Bilefeld, Germany.

by the importance that the jurist attaches to it) "something" of what the law seems by its very movement to be forgetting. As such, legal thought seems to have missed the question of the ordinary construction of a category. First of all, we should note the need to abandon a "semantic" conception of the construction of fundamental rights. Then, secondly, we should examine how this legal category is likely, from the perspective of the philosophy of ordinary language, to manifest a specific knotting of the real *in* legal language (in a specialised language).[6] Finally, it will be necessary to draw the consequences in law by uncovering hidden relationships between the fundamental and the important. What then comes into play is the reintegration of the subject of the legal statement into the legal statement (which is by nature blind to this presence). In our tradition, which is dominated by a certain normativist positivism, this presence is only virtual and thus masks the *virtue of the*[7] important under the guise of the fundamental.

1 A category of "fundamental rights" with no correlation with the world

This general approach requires, in our opinion, three preliminary clarifications: the legal thinking referred to is, naturally, that of jurists (i.e., those who develop a discourse *on* law and those who elaborate positive law *in the* very nature of its practice: the "legal operators"[8]); the "things" referred to are presented as "events" that[9] are made present in the discourse of law; finally, the "concepts"

6 This specialty language by its nature expresses an oversight of the position of the utterance, it is all in the inherent form of its utterance. It is thus constructed in relation to the foreclosure of any subject of the utterance. This foreclosure is countered by a certain empirical reading of the law. In this perspective: Éric MILLARD, *Théorie du droit*, Dalloz, Paris, 2006. Professor Millard quotes Jérôme Frank, (*Court son Trial,* Princeton University Press, 1949), who developed the famous formula that can account for the court decision D=PxS. In this formula (P) corresponds to the personality of the judge and (S) to the stimuli. Millard develops this formula as follows: AC=D because N (an act of concretisation is presented as a decision because of the presence of a norm). Furthermore, this norm is analysed in the following way: PxS=>N. The stimuli are understood in the following way: S = S(f) + S(cf) + S(inf) in this formula S(f) corresponds to formalised sources of enunciations; S(cf) to conformalised sources (sources to which one conforms) and S(inf) to informal sources such as ideology.

7 The virtual, as the etymology tells us, is the real manifestation of a force: it is by virtue of this that the fundamental as an element of the language of specialisation is efficient.

8 The legal operators that manifest themselves as essential in the realistic legal theory of law. For example, for an analysis in French of the thinking on this issue by the master of so-called moderate realistic thinking: Éric MILLARD. "Who are the 'legal operators' of Riccardo Guastini," *Analisi e Diritto*, (2014), pp. 103–113.

9 Cf. on this question – and beyond the debate on the definition of the concept of event – the references in note 11 on the distinction between objects and facts. There is a delicate relationship to be perceived between an event and the truth. This truth is ultimately what gives the event its sustenance. As such, truth is posited a *posteriori* as the cause of the event, whereas it is only the reason for it: its logical condition of possibility or existence (in the structure of this discourse).

offer conceptual content to the[10] reflection of jurists in the construction of their own world.

In this sense, to treat the issue of "fundamental rights" as referring to a "legal category" is to express the idea that the objects to which the extension of the legal concept refers could be the subject of a specific arrangement in the legal universe[11]: it is, therefore, a matter of ordering these objects (fundamental rights) and equipping oneself with a relevant apparatus vis-à-vis them.

In the light of these clarifications, the difficulty of thinking about this legal category seems to be clarified by the presence of two flaws: on the one hand, the idea of a representation and a relationship inherent in the concepts with regard to the world (1.1) and on the other hand, the desire to repel a certain skepticism through ideology (1.2).

1.1 The rejection of inherence

The question of the relationship between 'fundamental rights' – understood as a 'legal category' – and the social reality in which they develop is usually presented in the discourse on law as a main question. This demand is inherent in the historicity of the concepts[12] (and of the categories that are generated by the mobilisation of certain concepts)[13]. This evolution over time of "categories" and "concepts" is[14] merely an illustration of a confusion between the "concept" and

10 On this question, for example, J. BENOIST, *Le bruit du sensible*, Cerf, Paris, 2013.

11 The category is a concept whose specific function is to domesticate (in a certain way and through the mobilisation of concepts that are in some way secondary) a relationship to reality.

12 For example, M. TROPER, "Sur l'usage des concepts juridiques en histoire," *Annales Economies, Societies, Civilisations.* 47^{e} year, N. 6, 1992.

13 To begin with, let us agree on the following: our approach in this text articulates certain elements in the following way. 1.1. *Tractatus logico-philosophicus*: "The world is the totality of facts, not of things"; 2.034.*TLP:* "The structure of the fact consists in the structures of states of things"; 2.1.*TLP:* "We make images of facts"; 2.12 *TLP:* "The image is a model of reality"; 2.17. *TLP*: "What the image must have in common with reality in order to represent it in its own way – correctly or incorrectly – is its form of representation"; 2.225 *TLP:* "There is no a priori true image"; 3. *TLP*: "The logical image of facts is thought"; 3.1. *TLP*: "In the proposal thought is expressed for sensitive perception"]. These facts are thus the very matter of the world that language offers to sensibility: it is therefore a projection of thought. These facts, expressed in language, manipulate objects that are generated by language and language imposes, in this way, a grammatical necessity. Language imposes in its relation to the world categories that offer to classify these objects (3.22. *TLP*: "The name is in the proposition the representative of the object"; 3.3. *TLP*: "Only the proposition has a meaning; it is only linked in a proposition that the name has a meaning.") L. WITTGENSTEIN, *Tractatus logico-philosophicus,* Gallimard, Paris, 2001.

14 The category is thus only a specific concept. Concepts act by discriminating between things in the world in order to answer questions that the world asks about action or thought. In this sense, the category, understood as a species of the concept genre, offers to order our relationship to the world and to respond to the challenge of thinking or giving a logical image of it. Moreover, as a concept, the category is also led to

the "name" of the concept. It would express the presence of a job that would appear at best as awkward leading to talking about something different by referring to the same name.[15]

In these hypotheses, it would therefore be a matter of bringing together, on the one hand, a category which – in order to give us a grip on the world – must be understood as fixed and, on the other hand, a social reality which, for its part, is characterised by a certain fluidity and constructivism.[16] It is this classical approach, marked by the correspondence between the world and the category, that we shall challenge by contrasting a semantics of fundamental rights with a pragmatic

mobilise other concepts. As Wittgenstein notes: "concepts lead us to do research. They are the expression of our interest and direct it." L. WITTGENSTEIN, *Recherches philosophiques,* § 570: *Recherches philosophiques,* Gallimard, Paris, 2004.

15 In this text we depart from an analysis in which legal terms are understood within the framework of "atomistic" thinking in which "what is the case" [the facts] is the essential logical element. Within these facts lie, as we have just presented, the objects that are therefore inherent in them. It is thus the structure of the facts that offers to analyse them. These facts are then "states of things." From this perspective, the objects can only be postulated, because they are linked to the "state of things." It is this analysis that Professor O. develops, in line with Wittgenstein's *Tractatus*.PFERSMANN in his theoretical analysis dedicated to fundamental rights (*cf.* L. FAVOREU (ed.), *Droit des libertés fondamentales,* 1st ed., Dalloz, Paris, 2000, "Sketch of a theory of fundamental rights," pp. 89–142). Certain objects can thus only appear in certain states of affairs. The object is what the name refers to. In this approach, language is a representation or image of the world. Part of our departure from this analysis lies in the attention we wish to pay to various elements such as ordinary language a certain phenomenological approach to language and in the fact that the meaning is not in the object but in the use. This is a certain way of referring to the theories of ordinary language which have their origin in the work of the second Wittgenstein.

16 On these questions see N. Luhmann or G. Teubner. Among a very rich work, we will only mention (among the French publications) N. LUHMANN, *La confiance. Un mécanisme de réduction de la complexité sociale,* Economica, Paris, 2006; *La légitimation par la procédure,* PUL/Cerf, Paris, 2001. G. TEUBNER, *Le droit un système autopoïétique,* PUF, Paris, 1993. In this respect, in a sociological register Luhmann's analysis that fundamental rights understood as a legal sub-system fight against the deterioration of the complexity of social systems is essential. For the record, according to the German sociologist, society develops in accordance with the principles of specialisation and complexity. In this sense, it becomes increasingly complex and therefore develops sub-systems and these sub-systems become specialised. All systems are blind (because of the way they code themselves – by developing a theory inherent to what they are) to their real function for the benefit of society). For Luhmann, fundamental rights as a legal sub-system develop a function to fight against the regression of social complexity. Thus, the different generations of fundamental rights bear witness to the struggle of the social system against the hegemonic attempt of certain sub-systems: for example, the hegemony of the political or economic system … this approach opens up particularly rich perspectives with regard, for example, to the distinction between rights that protect from state intervention and rights that require state intervention … on the rights of the 3rd generation: D. MARRANI, "Reinforcing environmental rights: The French charter for the environment," *Revista Europea de Derechos Fundamentales primer semester,* 25 (2015), pp. 383–400. TURNER, S., SHELTON, D., RAZZAQUE, J., MCINTYRE, O. and MAY, J., eds, *Environmental rights: The development of standards,* Cambridge University Press, Cambridge, 2019.

approach to[17] them based on a form of life.[18] In order to do this, we will try to take advantage of recent contributions from the philosophy of ordinary language in an attempt to clarify certain notions inherent in the implementation of normative language.[19]

This question of the historicity of concepts is currently dealt with mainly in the context of reflexive law. Here there is an opposition between a law based on the application of the rule on the model of law (thus on the presence of a strong necessity) and on the other hand on the model of jurisprudence and reflexive law[20] (which manifests itself as the bearer of a more contingent necessity: what could be presented according to Leibniz's phrase as "an inclination without necessity"). What is presented in these hypotheses is ultimately the concept understood in a Hegelian perception:

> The bud disappears in the burst of flowering, and one could say that the bud is refuted by the flower: At the appearance of the fruit, too, the flower is denounced as a false being of the plant and the fruit is introduced instead of the flower as its truth. These forms are not only distinct, but also each one refutes the other, because they are mutually incompatible. But at the same time their fluid nature makes them moments of organic unity in which they not only repel each other, but in which one is as necessary as the other, and this equal necessity alone constitutes the life of the whole.[21]

17 On what is pragmatism as a philosophical movement: J.-P. COMETTI, *What is pragmatism?* Gallimard, Paris, 2010.

18 That is, finally, to an ordinary way of following a rule. This is a presentation of the rule that challenges a mythological conception of the rule in the classical form of rails that would give rise to a form of necessity. This is what is usually presented as the sceptical conception of the rule. However, it would be wrong to think that we mean nothing in the language and in its use. There is, in Wittgenstein's words, "an understanding of the rule that is not an interpretation" of a community agreement or practice [§ 201 of *Philosophical Research*]. We agree not so much on meanings as on ordinary usage: a background of exhaustive and systematic agreements as CAVELL [of life forms] observes in *A New America Still Unreachable*, L'éclat, Paris, 1993. If the language is given, the mystery remains as to how I will tune in with the others in it. However, this agreement is not intersubjective, it is fully objective: what cannot be taken out of it is life as it usually unfolds. Language can mean nothing other than this ordinary of the world in which it obviously develops. What is constant in man is the fact that he is a speaking being and therefore unable to leave language is the natural history of man and the anthropological aspect of man's own grammar.

19 We are referring, of course, to Wittgenstein (the *philosophical researcher*), Austin and Cavell. In France this current is represented mainly by S. Laugier.

20 European Union law is a perfect example of this conceptual work. Professor Azoulai thus indicated that Union law has no language of its own and that it uses the languages of others: in this sense the nature of Union law is particularly open to iteration and deconstruction. L. AZOULAI, "La limite à l'arrêt. Positivité de la transgression chez J. Derrida," in *La transgression*, Bruylant, Bruxelles, 2013, p. 504.

21 G.W.F. HEGEL, *Genèse et structure de la Phénoménologie de l'esprit*, Vol. 1, Aubier, Paris, 1946, p. 366.

This mission is, however, particularly delicate to implement. In fact, legal thinking often fails to provide a real analysis of the effort to categorise and focuses only on the benefits derived from such implementation (for example, the inclusion of values in the legal order). There is, in this way, a blind spot with regard to the inherent category of fundamental rights.[22] The various attempts to construct the category through the efforts of the doctrine are in the end rather disappointing.[23] The epistemological approach thus easily gives way to ideology.[24] Fundamental rights in this perspective appear either as a limit to power or as a foundation.[25]

In general, the analysis of the category in the legal field remains relatively trivial. The treatment offered by the law gives precedence to a definition by *extension to the* detriment of a definition by the *understanding of the* concept mobilised by the category in question. This approach indicates that the category is apprehended as a "sum" and[26] not as having a prior "unit." This is an application linked to the classic distinction between *extension* and *understanding that is* specific to concepts.

22 This is the case for other legal categories (if not all legal categories), however, when it comes to fundamental rights, the denial is perhaps even more blatant because of the particularism and importance currently offered to fundamental rights in relation to contemporary constitutionalism.

23 The list of attempts is too large to be exhaustive. We will limit ourselves to exhausting the strategies that are generally developed by the doctrine to achieve this definition. Generally speaking, there are three strategies: (1) a strategy by extension; (2) a substantial definition (fundamental rights are those that have a certain content) – a characteristic approach is that of C. Schmitt, for whom fundamental rights are not all constitutionally established rights, but only the rights of liberty) – also linked to this strategy is the idea of considering as fundamental rights only those that protect the interests that are considered important from the point of view of their holders or from an ethical or political position (this logic is found in the theoretical construction of R. Schmitt's theory). Dworkin's theoretical construction), finally, to this definition are attached the constructions that deduce the fundamentality of the category of holders (for example would be fundamental the universal rights attributed to all (for example, L. Ferrajoli); (3) a formal definition that focuses its attention on the rank of the norms that confer the right in the hierarchy of norms (the problem being, on the one hand, that this *a priori hierarchy does not* exist and that there are really only operations of hierarchisation carried out by legal operators in the confrontation of various norms and, on the other hand, that the hierarchy itself (or hierarchisation) is a complex concept that combines various hierarchies: axiological, formal, material, logical: on these questions R. Dworkin's definition of the hierarchy of norms is based on the following point: the hierarchy of norms is a complex concept, which is the result of the fact that the hierarchy of norms is not a hierarchy, but a hierarchy of rights, which is the result of the confrontation of various norms. GUASTINI, *Le fonti del diritto. Fondamenti teorici*, Giuffrè, Milano, 2010, pp. 241–254.

24 Ideology in the sense of Marxist "false consciousness" [according to which a reality, for Marxists naturally a dialectical reality, presents itself as distorted or disfigured. This concept has its origin in the book *German Ideology*]. Ideology acts to structure the sense of reality in individuals.

25 Pour une analyse lumineuse sur cette dualité: M. LUCIANI, "Constitutionalismo irenico e costituzionalismo polemico," in *Giurisprudenza costituzionale*, 2 (2006), pp. 1643–1668.

26 This is why the categories are regularly enriched by the jurisprudential work and are finally only the continuous action of the latter.

This choice of an *extension* approach reflects the desire to ensure that a certain pragmatism prevails in the development of the concept inherent to the category. Generally speaking, the law uses this approach, mainly by means of the regular construction of the category through the creative effort of case law, but does not *think so* (this is not its function: while the legal literature has the capacity to develop a certain definition or understanding of the concept, it does not have the power to generate it as an object of law, and case law, which has the power – through an act of will – to bring out the concept, does not have the power to think so). To succeed in transforming this sum into an *a priori* concept the jurist generally uses the reference to an "argument of authority." He uses a signifier that elicits adherence and has the value of being what other signifiers are not. In this way, the liberties that flow into legal discourse become "fundamental," just as certain requirements become "imperative" in other legal fields. To put it simply, the jurist generates reasons which, with retroactive performativity, then appear in their own order (positive law) as causes. It is in this respect that positive law acts fully as the screen on which certain issues of social reality are played out and the screen that inscribes the latter as its internal limit.

This category of fundamental rights is presented as a kind of "language game" that ultimately explains its imprecision. This language game[27] differs, however, from the classical forms of games (in the common sense). Indeed, it applies to reality and not totally to the institution it engenders.[28] Once it has been stated that law is not in a "correlationist" relationship with the world, but that it participates in its making, a second bias must be ruled out: that of ideology.[29]

27 Wittgenstein's idea of language games takes the following form: in *The Notes on Private Experience and Data Senses* he says: "We call something a language game if it plays a special role in our human life." See *Notes on Private Experience and Sense Data*, Blackwell, Oxford, 1980. It is therefore a question of accounting for the interweaving of language and an activity (of a form of life: the customs of the language community).

28 As observed by C. Cavaillé: "the examination and exercise of language games change our way of seeing and solicit personal thought; they are conceptual and demanding, but they show that the ability to conceptualise is inherent in ordinary real life and that it is always within our reach to make explicit and manifest what is important." C. CAVAILLÉ, *Les jeux de language chez Wittgenstein,* Demopolis, Paris, 2016, p. 8.

29 With the question of ideology comes the question of truth inherent in the discourse of the jurist as a legal operator who, through acts of will, generates positive law. The jurist prefers to know it to the truth. In a way, his discourse is always marked by metonymy, i.e., by a full discourse and he ignores its metaphorical scope (i.e., a discourse that is open to a certain emptiness: to a gap). From the perspective of the creation of law by degree, for example, which is the dominant paradigm of our presentation of law, this idea of an autonomous law and a full discourse clearly manifests itself. The terms of the problem are well known. Under the gradualist theory norms have a higher norm as a necessary (but not sufficient) condition of validity and are the necessary but not sufficient condition of the lower norm. In the lowest degree standards are validated, but not valid. In the highest degree the standard validates the whole, but is not validated. Therefore, in the degree creation theory of the legal system, the fundamental norm is either not valid or not fundamental: it is not valid if it is fundamental, because, hypothetically, there is no higher norm that can validate it; it is not fundamental if it is valid, since, by definition, it is valid only if it is validated by another higher norm. To respond

1.2 The rejection of skepticism

In this sense, the question is the following: what does the statement "fundamental rights" really *mean* – and beyond this relationship of meaning that it is the orientation between the category (the classifying concept) and the world?[30] Why do we, in law, conceptualise the social world on the basis of this classifying concept? Why, in implementing this category of fundamental rights, do I sometimes have the feeling that I have "hit the nail on the head" or "missed the world"[31]: and this "as if" in the use of legal language I had sometimes properly grasped the very articulation of reality? If the world is nothing more than a conceptual reality (if we are responsible for the development of the format), how can we grasp this feeling that there is a necessary constraint present in the way we refer to this same reality?

Far from a certain idea that "true" thought or experience must conform and correspond to a reality (truth in this sense is not a correspondence to the world, but a property of the sentence), it must be understood that the thought of reality (or experience) is, in fact, normalised by our thoughts. Fundamental rights exist only within the framework of the state of things that makes them exist (the category that mobilises certain concepts and presents these objects). The meaning of "fundamental rights" (as the generic name for objects) is inferred from the use that will commonly be made of these objects in the ordinary course of legal practice, through concepts that, by their nature, are intended to address certain problems.

To sum up: the "category" classifies and orders; the "objects" are linked to the state of things; the more or less complex "names" and "statements" express the structure of the state of things in a language. O. Pfersmann, for example, has focused on this useful clarification in the above-mentioned text. "Concepts," for example, appear when it comes to responding to a challenge that our relationship to the world poses to us at a certain point in time;[32] this challenge explains the regular enrichment of the category by the formation of new concepts.

to this situation it is possible to play on the terms of the problem or on the criteria inherent in the problem. It is thus possible to challenge this theory by adhering, for example, to jus naturalistic analyses. Finally, it is possible to focus on the criteria. In this sense, the thesis that denies the idea that the validity of the fundamental norm must be proven according to the same criteria as those that underpin the proof of the validity of other norms, and that the validity of the fundamental norm is postulated by the gradualist theory of the system itself. In this perspective depending on whether in the agreement on the criteria I agree on the presence of a thesis or a hypothesis the answer will be different. The metaphor, on the other hand, reappears the idea of a certain justice or, more precisely, a certain silence of the law and therefore an inherent deviation from the law.

30 Classically, the philosophy of normative language considers that the relationship between legal language through its categories or concepts and the world can be analogical or catalogical (a reflection of the world or a shaping of the world).

31 This feeling of having lost the world or of being unable to have a true experience of it and through language is what is presented in philosophy as skepticism.

32 A colleague recently during a thesis defence in Dakar gave me his specific approach to the relations between concepts and notions: for him, a concept is a (conceptual) framework and notions are what is presented in this framework in the reflection it offers.

Thought inscribed in language thus determines the format inherent in our encounter with reality or with the real.[33] It does not presuppose a connection to the world; it *expresses* this connection in the application of the category, in its use. It thus formulates the presence of a standard expressed in a practice. It appears as a particular knot between the language of the speciality that uses it and the world in which this language is used.[34] This situation was perfectly apprehended by Wittgenstein during the transition he makes, in the second part of his work, between "grammar"[35] and "forms of life." This is not a *semantic* turning point, but a desire to anchor grammatical necessity not to a reality that is pre-existing – and upstream – but to a meaning that is downstream of usage. As Wittgenstein observes, the grammatical approach is a kind of struggle against our tendency to imagine that we have to penetrate phenomena. The classical perception of a category, for example in Kant, manifests this need to penetrate and catch the real, whereas grammatical perception implies an experience in use. In this sense, with fundamental rights I don't catch any social reality, but I express an experience.[36]

2 A category of "fundamental rights" *expressing what is* important at the human level

In constructing this legal category of fundamental rights there is agreement and agreement on criteria (2.1). These express an agreement on what is important, which implies rethinking various legal problems that appear, in a classical approach, insoluble (2.2).

2.1 An agreement on criteria

An agreement in the important and not in the fundamental. In the construction of a category, according to a famous formula, it is a question of agreeing *in* use on criteria and not on a meaning.

The criterion is "what determines the judgment or decision at the point of application of the speech act, according to what is important in the particular circumstances."[37] It appears that it is therefore through the criteria that one

33 On this question: J. BENOIST, *L'adresse du réel*, Vrin, Paris, 2017. From the same author, *Concepts: introduction to analysis, collection passages*, Cerf, Paris, 2010.

34 Mutual understanding through language requires not only agreement on definitions, but also (strange as it may seem) agreement in judgments. This seems to abolish logic, but it does not. It is one thing to describe a method of measurement, and quite another to find and formulate the results of a measurement. But what we call 'measuring' is also determined by a certain consistency in the outcome of the measurements. L. WITTGENSTEIN, *Recherches philosophiques*, § 242.

35 With the grammatical turn Wittgenstein begins to turn his back on any theory of knowledge. It is not a question of knowing (of establishing a relationship to the world), but only of making oneself heard on the basis of statements that make sense.

36 We will see that the specificity of this experience is the feeling of what is important.

37 C. CAVAILLÉ, *op. cit.*, p. 68. The criteria are a bit like the symptoms of agreement.

determines whether what is being dealt with is "the case."[38] This question is essential, because contrary to a common perception that concepts provide a framework for implementing criteria[39] (this is the "official" approach to criteria); *a contrario,* in an ordinary conception of language, criteria teach us what the concepts are: this inversion, which is masked by the practice of positive law, constitutes our agreement and experience of the ordinary. It should

38 This question is largely present in the reflections of the second Wittgenstein. He approaches the criteria on a grammatical basis. Two fragments from the Austrian philosopher's work can thus be mobilised for the benefit of the understanding of this notion. According to § 373 of the *RP* and § 580 of the *RP*: according to the first, "it is grammar that tells us what kind of object is something" and according to the second, "an internal process needs external criteria." As S. CAVELL has made clear (*Wittgenstein, Les voix de la raison, scepticism, morality and tragedy*, Seuil, Paris, 1996, especially Chapter 1, 'Criteria and judgment'), Wittgenstein distinguishes between ordinary and official criteria. In the official approach there are two means (the norms and the criteria) by which a group judges and selects membership of a certain status: the norms determine the degree to which the candidate meets the criteria, and the criteria determine whether the object in question is of the right kind. Thus, there are formal criteria for determining whether the object "must be fundamental" falls within the category "fundamental right" and standards for assessing the degree of membership in the category. From this perspective, the criteria are what allow the questioning to be *stopped* and *certainty to be* rooted. The official approach refers to 7 criteria:

(1) the source of the authority (e.g., the legislator, the settlor, etc.);
(2) the modality of exercise of the authority (e.g., the institution of a status, a state of affairs by law ...);
(3) the epistemic aim (for example, to judge or to institute);
(4) the candidate object or phenomenon (a category, a definition, a concept ...);
(5) the concept that defines status (its quality: for example, for a standard, its validity);
(6) the epistemic means (for the concept, its understanding and extension);
(7) the degree of satisfaction (it is a test that allows the previous criterion to be applied: thus, for example, the argumentation and the reflexivity that it implies on the case and the concept).

In the name of the mobilization of these criteria a legal operator can thus determine with certainty (for him) that a thing falls into a category. The thing being understood with certainty (the existence of fundamental rights) it is finally a question of determining according to what degree the case belongs to the thing (is it in this case a "fundamental right"?). This differentiation does not exist in the ordinary application of the criteria for Wittgenstein according to Cavell. For Wittgenstein, there is no decisive criterion in the ordinary application of the criteria for Wittgenstein. Moreover, according to this ordinary approach the object and the concept (criteria 4 and 5) are in a singular position. Indeed, in the ordinary approach there is no a priori identification of the concept and there is no a priori identification of its quality. In the official approach, a norm, for example, implies a definition, and it is from this definition (in and by positive law within the framework of positivism) that its quality will be apprehended: its existence in the order of law, that is to say, its validity. In the ordinary there is no clear question of evaluation or status.

39 Internal experience thus needs external criteria.

be understood that according to this approach language is always "said" in a context and as such necessarily expressed by a human voice.[40]

This leads to the idea that the criteria on which we agree in ordinary usage (ordinary grammar) of fundamental rights – from what is or is not important in the ordinary of a form of life – are the basis of our understanding of fundamentality. Fundamentality would, in this way, only be the translation of what is important in a life form to people in a specific context and what our agreement on criteria expresses. This is by no means trivial, because the legal translation of this situation erases an essential dimension of fundamental rights as objects and as an ordinary concept: it postulates a concept and deduces from it an agreement in its criteria. In this sense, the legal translation of the problem is based on a stipulative fiction.

The ordinary language philosophy we use to refine the fundamental rights approach questions the relationship between language and the world "differently," starting from the problem traditionally presented as "skepticism"[41] (does the world exist outside and independently of language?). It offers, in its own way, to reconcile the jurist with a certain sense of justice (or more precisely of rightness) with regard to the world in which he or she works. This analysis thus has a clear impact on the acceptance of the notions, concepts, definitions, categories, etc. that normative language elicits – or at least seeks to elicit.

The contribution of the philosophy of ordinary language is to demonstrate that, in the end, this question is impassable and that there is no answer to skepticism, but a necessary acceptance, fully integrated, to be realised, and this, because skepticism is part of our human form of life. There is, in the very fact of being men (talking animals), the inscription of skepticism as a fact that the question of the relationship to the world and the relationship to the other is always fragile, because it is necessarily apprehended through language. Taking this skepticism into account therefore implies making it a real experience.

To speak of "fundamental rights," *in* accordance with this orientation, is therefore to establish a specific relationship to the world and more precisely to the world itself through legal practice. It is the implementation of a "language game" that nevertheless only makes sense within a "form of life," i.e., a complex set of relationships inherent in activity and life. This constitutive and inherent grammar of our form of life is autonomous and does not seem to be based on any *a priori*

40 See, S. LAUGIER, "Presentation," Stanley Cavell, *Revue internationale de philosophie*, 2 (2011), p. 114. This analysis explains why Cavell's book, *The Claim of Reason*, was translated in France as: *Les voix de la raison*.

41 It is Kripke who seems to have found in Wittgenstein this radical presence of scepticism that there is not one fact that could provide a foundation for what we understand as a concept. S. KRIPKE, *Rules and Private Language. Introduction au paradoxe de Wittgenstein*, Seuil, Paris, 1996. For Cavell, criteria are not a condition of assertion that fixes the certainty of our statements, but the conditions of our possession of language: there is no *reason for* their existence, but what makes them exist is that we finally share a certain sense of what is important at a certain moment and in a certain context.

real "fact" (this would obviously be contrary to the very idea of grammar: a fact is only what could be the "case" *in* a grammar and with *regard to* a grammar).

As the *Tractatus* indicates, formal concepts, such as the "meaning" of the name of an object (for us fundamental rights), when understood as ingredients or elements of the world cannot be the subject of semantic formulation: they do not appear to be "signifiers" and *ultimately* relate to what Wittgenstein presents as "nonsense." They thus express purely grammatical knowledge. The concept mobilised by the category does not show anything of the world; it does, however, offer to see something in the world in relation to a problem: a "something" (the objects elaborated from the conceptual framework) which is "the case" of this concept and which is grammatically related to it.

The recent success of the mainly academic legal approach linked to case analysis can be deduced from this (more or less) awareness. In this sense, in the world of fundamental rights there would not be fundamental rights that would be targeted *a priori* by reference, but there would be a state of affairs based on grammar and the language game posed in a form of life from the category of fundamental rights that could be identified in this way: the essence of fundamental rights would thus be grammatically the state of affairs that is at issue in the status of fundamental rights would not be *a priori*. To quote the philosopher Jocelyn Benoist: "grammar is only the law of truth … or, more generally, of the normalised encounter of reality in language."[42] In Professor A's own terminology, Conte is then a question of differentiating a semantic conception of the utterance which is not athetical but thetical: that is to say, it is posed in reference to the utterance itself. The syntactic conception would also be thetical: it would be reduced to the classical conception of validity for a jurist and would be posed by the very nature of positive law.

The pragmatic conception seems more interesting with regard to our approach: is the validity of the act of language as practice formed by reference to a concept immanent to the statement or by reference to a hypothetico-constitutive rule? It seems to us that, when the category is rooted in a certain "morality," the answer lies in what Conte presents as praxeonomic validity (therefore with reference to a hypothetico-constitutive external rule); whereas in the ordinary approach the validity of the category would be praxeological, i.e., constructed by fidelity to the very concept of the utterance: agreement in the criteria of what a community in a form of life considers important.[43] This analysis implies a clarification of the relationship between the criteria and the concept.

More precisely, and in accordance with the distinction between official and ordinary criteria, the fundamental rights recognised by positive law are recognised on the basis of a distinction between criteria and norms which plays differently in the two hypotheses (official and ordinary): in official usage, the legal operator

42 J. BENOIST, *L'adresse du réel*, Vrin, Paris, 2017, p. 162.

43 On these analyses Amedeo G. CONTE, *Studio per una teoria della validità* (1970), in A. G. CONTE,*Filosofia del linguaggio normativo. I. Studi 1965–1981*, Giappichelli, Torino, 1995, pp. 55–74. For a translation and commented analysis: P. RICHARD and L. PASSERINI GLAZEL, *Philosophie du language normatif, anthology of texts by A. G. Conte*, PUL, Quebec, 2020,

brings a norm into play on the basis of criteria which are implicit for him (it is the characteristic of positive law to rely in this way in order to be applied on a tautology – law is what law recognises as law – which is admitted without being questioned).

Ordinary language, for its part, shows that in the constitution of the grammar of fundamental rights in their ordinary use (i.e., as soon as law and litigation are integrated into the very life of societies and are recognised as having a social function) these two dimensions of judgement telescope: in the way – always different and fragile – of presenting them, it is apparent that the ordinary of life is always being manufactured in the negotiation of one another's claims. It is easy from this clarification to understand that the official translation of law can only be received as legitimate by a society when it is properly articulated with ordinary usage. In addition to the syntactic validity expressed by the law (e.g., the normativist conception), there is also a semantic validity and a pragmatic validity that is illuminated by this ordinary approach to legal language and its statements.

If the category of "fundamental rights" thus refers to nothing more than a grammatical constraint inscribed in a form of life, then it should be given serious consideration. This constraint will take the form of a rule that norms the category. It is thus presented as the constitutive rule inherent in the category in question. This identification overlaps with that between the rules which allow the definition of an activity in the broad sense and the rules which express a constraint specific to reality or a relationship to reality. This is the famous distinction between regulatory rules and constituent rules. Naturally, the ontological relationship (or the ontological density relative to what is regulated is different). This question of the presence of a constitutive rule has been perfectly dealt with recently by a Polish phenomenologist.[44]

44 Wojciech Elaniec, "On the idea of constitutive norms." "We have said that by moving a bishop without doing it diagonally, we violate a rule of chess, and this in a very similar way to what happens when we lie, or violate a rule of human communication, in the same way that when we take more or less water (or milk), we violate a recipe. However, it may be that the difference between the two types of cases lies in the fact that a piece of wood must first be constituted as "mad," whereas an assertion in a certain context is at first sight a communication, and not only because it has been constituted as such. This seems to be the crux of the distinction elaborated in Rawls' pioneering text "two concepts of rules": rules of regulation regulate the behaviour of existing objects independently of them, whereas constitutive rules create or modify objects, whose behaviour may or may not be regulated afterwards. The rule that the bishop must move only diagonally, whatever it is, presupposes the concept of the bishop in chess. And there is another rule which says that a bishop is what is found in C1, F1, C8 and F8. But then another rule tells us that chess must be played on a board of eight squares by eight. And yet another rule tells us that when you start playing chess – or as they say, when you start "a game of chess" – the squares from A1 to H2 inclusive, and those from A7 to H8 inclusive are occupied. So here is the first rule – the one that states that things that occupy certain spaces are called "bishops," or the rule that what occupies those spaces must be called "bishop." Rules of this type state what must happen before a game of chess can begin. Once again one cannot escape the similarity with the first sentences of a recipe for cooking food, which usually say things like: "Take the water or milk, wheat flour, salt and sugar, pour it into a pot and add the eggs." However,

With "fundamental rights," it is therefore not a question of appending our language to a pre-existing reality of which it is merely the transposition or pure representation – it is a question of determining a regulated use of this grammatical statement in a "form of life." Reality is, in this perspective, only the very use of language: the very life of this use. In fact, is it possible to get out of language? What is real is the very use of language in the ordinary course of its practice. What is real is what "I"[45] reveals (what I show) in litigation: what "I" shows is that certain things in the ordinary life of the protagonists of the social game are "important."[46] There are things that I cannot not know and there are things that I cannot not say.

To state that certain things are important in this way is to emphasise an expressive "knot" within a life form. What is important is what manifests itself through the "natural" agreement on criteria: what everyone cannot fail to know.[47] What is essentially important is what is obvious: obviousness. If language is *our* way of encountering the world, then this obviousness is important for *everyone*. The determination in litigation, for example, of what is important to each person (the claims) is presented as an *expressive* rationality (a specific rationality that is distinct from scientific rationality and that is justified in a singular way) making visible the agreement in and on a "form of life."[48]

Ordinary agreement does not account for the truth of the judgement or its correspondence to a state of affairs, but only for the *quality of the* enunciator's world in language. The importance as claimed in the dispute makes visible, in a way, the threshold of obviousness that characterises agreement in a form of life. In a way, litigation in which fundamental rights are at stake is an opportunity to experience what is important. It should be pointed out here that it is not so much a matter of explaining or describing it. In some ways, disputes in which fundamental rights are at stake are an opportunity to experience what is important. It is not only a matter of explaining or describing that experience, but of questioning its possibility.[49] The experience of fundamental rights thus appears as an adventure of the attention of the legal operators in order to reach the experience of what is

unlike these rules, chess rules of the kind mentioned above are completely abstract. Wojciech ELANIEC, "Sull'idea stessa di regola costitutiva," in P. DI LUCIA, *Ontologia sociale Potere deontico e regole costitutiva,* Quodlibet, Macerata, 2003, pp. 155–179.

45 Because of the nature of skepticism, it is always an individual inscribed in language who tries to inscribe his pretension in a relationship with the other.

46 On this question of importance in the thought of Wittgenstein and S. Cavell: S. LAUGIER, "L'importance de l'importance: expérience, pragmatisme, transcendentalisme," *Multitudes,* 4 (23) (2005), pp. 153–167.

47 This question is perhaps not far removed from certain contemporary approaches to legal theory that attempt to re-found the law in a modernised natural law based on the concept of common property. In this sense, J. Finnis characterizes the latter as what I cannot but want. This instance in the formula on negations manifests, in our view, the presence of this necessity inherent in a form of life. J. FINNIS, *Natural Law and Natural Rights,* Clarendon, Oxford, 1980.

48 In the context of a dispute, the legal operators will defend positions, claims. They will share with the interlocutors a form of evidence.

49 S. LAUGIER, "L'importance de l'important," *op. cit.,* p. 158.

important: what really matters, that is to say, the nuances of the experience. This is perhaps what currently explains the influence of the "principles" in the litigation experience of fundamental rights: by their very nature, these imply a balancing, a weighting and therefore a nuanced and proportionate application.[50]

2.2 An agreement on materiality

It is understandable that this analysis offers a solution to various problems traditionally linked to the use of the category of fundamental rights and which could disappear in the register of ordinary language philosophy.

The question of fundamentality: this can be summed up in this perspective as an analysis of the grammaticality of the form of life. It is the latter that is fundamental in this very particular sense, where it does not foundationalise anything, but offers language to develop in its practice. It would also be necessary to reintegrate the value of importance (of the concept of "important") in its rightful place and to abandon a false perception (or a second perception, because it is inherent in a certain legal language game always haunted by a search for foundations) specific to the category of fundamentality.

The question of the historicity of the concepts which seems inherent to the category of fundamental rights: the questioning boils down to examining the relationships between the concepts and their uses in a language game present at the heart of a form of life. A full awareness of skepticism would make it possible to abandon futile debates on the *a priori* or *a posteriori* aspects of concepts and their analogical or catalogical relationships to the world.[51]

The question of the hierarchy of fundamental rights: this question is presented in the logic of ordinary language in the form of the study of the status of the samples.[52] In this sense, fundamental rights would not be hierarchical, but would be ordered on the basis of fundamental rights that might better than others present themselves as relevant samples of the category in question. The sample would thus be a characteristic ideal type. This approach would make it possible to better situate the plurality of legal hierarchies as presented in the legal analyses. Professor Guastini[53] has demonstrated perfectly that hierarchy develops along four dimensions: axiological, material, formal, logical, etc. and that it is not given, but constructed through the use of norms and statements by legal operators (it would thus be appropriate to speak not of hierarchies, but of hierarchisations). Finally, is

50 It is in the manifestation of this attention to the ordinary that literature is perhaps most needed in law. Indeed, it expresses and endeavors to manifest and make visible what is important in the ordinary of a story. This attention must also be perceptible in legal literature: in the specific way in which the protagonists of a dispute express what matters most to them in the conversation about justice that they engage in with the judge in the context of an argumentative space.

51 An analogical rule *is* the condition of what it sets, whereas a catalogical rule *sets* the condition of what it regulates.

52 On this question: N. GOODMAN, *Manières de faire des mondes*, Chambon, Paris, 1992.

53 See *infra* note 20.

this approach not the translation of the fact that some objects are presented in the context of litigation as better samples than others on the basis of the criteria on which we agree (the official judgment thus applies on the basis of implicit criteria a norm or standard that will make it possible to assess the degree to which the object of the claim belongs to the conceptual category offered by the criteria).

The question of the definition by understanding and a priori *of the category of fundamental rights*: It would be advisable to abandon an approach of this type, which remains semantic, in favour of a more pragmatic analysis according to which the definition would be reduced to the sum of uses and therefore to a definition by extension – and therefore *a posteriori* – and to draw the consequences. This pragmatic approach offers, for its part, to settle another essential question related to the *normativity of categories and concepts*: necessity being (in this model) grammatical, it is associated with the accepted way of constructing our reality: there is, in this framework, only conceptual and grammatical necessity (and it should be added that grammatical necessity is that of a form of life: it is always to be reconstructed and fabricated, which explains the inherent gradualness of normativity).[54]

What is shown in this grammar is, finally, the fact that the utterance and its meaning are of the order of the performance of language (and thus its use) and that it questions *experience* (and an experience that has a tragic tonality) and the adventure inherent in the encounter with what is important in a form of life at a given moment in time. The pragmatic dimension then becomes essential and goes beyond a more classical approach, which is still partly haunted by a certain metaphysics and is presented in semantics. Fundamental rights litigation is thus the framework of a singular experience that needs to be detailed.

Finally, in our view, it is necessary to distinguish two dimensions present in the implementation of this legal category. Understandably, the analysis that has just been developed with regard to the legal category manifests the following idea: both the category and the concept allow language to deal with what seems outside of it (our biased relationship to social reality). More precisely, it offers to challenge the very idea of a separation between the world and the way it is presented in language. The construction of legal categories is fully an expression of our singular and evolving way of *accounting for the* fact that the world *matters to* us in a certain way. It is therefore in the world that this category otherwise *means,* but more accurately *expresses* its *meaning* (i.e., the way in which, in relation to this experience, "I" orientates myself in the world).

The category of fundamental rights thus offers the opportunity for a unique experience: to experience what is important and from this to think about the small differences and nuances of social life.[55]

54 It is this reality that S. Cavell expresses in the reflections developed in relation to so-called remarriage comedies in American cinema.

55 As such, it seems useful to refer to the "principle of charity" or "equivalence" as formalised by Davidson – and which in its own way imposes the idea, fairly classical in the field of psychoanalysis, according to which the subject is subject for a signifier and then finds meaning only in the Other of the structure of language. Davidson adheres to a

In the very end of his book on *Voices of Reason* (the part dealing with skepticism and the problem of others between recognition and avoidance), S. Cavell illustrates, in our view, perfectly this possibility of an inquiry into the importance and nuances it implies in a judicial setting. He places two fragments of thought in parallel: the first belongs to Hegel and is derived from the *philosophy of law,* while the second is by Nietzche and is to be found in *Ainsi parlait Zarathoustra* ["Of the pale criminal"]:

> Instead of the offended party, it is now the universal offended party that enters the scene, and ... assumes the prosecution and punishment of the crime, which thus ceases to be subjective and contingent reprisals ... and becomes the authentic reconciliation of law with itself, that is to say, in punishment. From the objective point of view, there is a reconciliation of the law with itself; through the annulment of the crime, the law re-establishes itself and realises its own authority. And from the subjective point of view, there is reconciliation of the criminal with himself, that is, with the law recognised as his own, as valid for him too, for his protection; and he himself finds, therefore, in the application of this law which he undergoes, the satisfaction of justice, and consequently, an action which is his own.
>
> Won't you kill, O judges and priests, before the beast has nodded its head? Behold, he has nodded his head, the pale criminal, and in his eye one reads great contempt.

In the analysis – and the comparison – of these two texts, all the nuances that make the moment of the trial *important are* thus apparent. It can be the moment of reconciliation or the moment of the criminal's punishment. The criminal's expressive nod can be acquiescence to the punishment or "the lowering of the head, which can just as easily signify defeat as announcing the attack."[56] Research on fundamental rights as a category of what is important implies, in this way, a resistance to this response to the skepticism illustrated by the search for fundamentality on the part of those involved in the trial. There is no fact that would be likely to form the basis of our criteria, but an agreement on what is important, which is always fragile and which critical thinking offers by its nuances to invigorate and reassure.

holistic conception of language: for him language is the whole Other. This holistic approach implies that the meaning is indeterminate and that it is extended to all the occurrences of the word within a discourse. It is therefore necessary to look at how the word functions in the order of discourse. In this logic, language does not *really* exist (it is only an ontological mirage), only the *factory of* meaning exists: understanding is thus interpreting the other's statements. When I interpret "I" is inclined to accept the idea of a systematic agreement of our beliefs and "I" accepts that in the place of the Other the meaning is thus deposited. The meaning of the concept is therefore the norm of my agreement with the Other and others.

56 S. CAVELL, *Les voix de la raison, op. cit.,* p. 670.

This analysis implies that the truth of this agreement results in the real acceptance of the following situation: not only can we not get out of language, but it is also impossible to reintegrate into discourse – whether specialised or not, but even more so in a specialised discourse such as that of jurists, which aims to give certainties and the impression that we can effectively act on the world – the part of enunciation. What Cavell expresses, in his own way, in the difficulty of making one's voice heard and speaking on behalf of the other.

What this distinction between what is fundamental and what is important suggests is this relationship and this loss: since the legal statement and the cause of its enunciation in ordinary language will never perfectly coincide. To weave the metaphor, we will say that in language and in legal language we are prisoners of a bottle of Klein and that we thus have the impression of passing from the inside to the outside, whereas we never leave the bottle (in fact, more precisely with the bottle of Félix Klein there is paradoxically no inside of the bottle).

The importance of a social enunciation in transforming itself into law under the regime of the fundamental makes the instance of enunciation deadlocked, which then appears as the grain of sand that will give consistency to our skepticism. This category of the fundamental in law thus offers to highlight ethical concepts and nuances that place life at the very heart of the experience and that by the attention given to them offer to agree on what is important. Fundamental rights could therefore be what offers a "voice" to the experience of the important. In this way, they would express an illustration of what Cavell describes as moral perfectionism, questioning the intertwining of words and the world. When Wittgenstein asserts that our tuning is *in* language and not *about* language, he manifests, according to Cavell, the idea that tuning is never intersubjective. It is in the sense that, for example, some like Habermas mean social connection and public space … or continued democracy), but more accurately manifests harmony (in the sense of musical chord) between individual voices – claims: i.e., ways of making one's voice heard – which exist and are valid only through their effort at universalisation: an experience of democracy not as a regime, but as an inquiry into its own nature.[57]

The point here is to articulate the impossible relationship between two elements: on the one hand, the voice that seeks to be heard in the agreement of a form of life, and on the other hand, the tragedy that[58] ultimately is the place within which one cannot escape the consequences of an overlapping of a question that is important to "us" by the other (the subject of the utterance and the subject of the utterance that disappears and always appears as other). In litigation, this tragic dimension manifests itself in the difficulty of bringing these two events together: what matters to me, cannot escape the grip of the presence of the other. The fundamental rights dispute is the most acute moment when skepticism thus

57 In the sense of pragmatism. In pragmatism there is an experience of democracy that occurs on the margins of institutions and powers. J.-P. COMETTI, *What is pragmatism? op. cit.,* p 40.

58 On this question of tragedy and comedy in the light of agreement: the two works by S. CAVELL*Dire et vouloir dire, op. cit.* and *A la recherche du bonheur, Hollywood et la Comédie de remariage,* Vrin, Paris, 2017.

meets the ordinary in an experience. For the parties, it is the moment of a necessary effort to pay attention to what is important. For institutions and commentators, it is the place for a specific ethical effort: to bring our sense of nuance into play. Fundamental rights as categories are thus devices that offer the opportunity to bring ethics into *play in* context (the context of their contentious implementation concerned with respect for the voice of the other). Through the contentious questioning that arises when fundamental rights are mentioned, the always fragile agreement on what is important to us is expressed. In this sense, legal language is a manifestation of the fact that it is fully a structure of the outside world, as Iris Murdoch observes[59] and as the logic of Klein's bottle illustrates in its own way.

In this dialectic between the fundamental and the important, we believe that the lawyer's relationship between the sign and the ordinary of the word is at stake. When the jurist forgets or denies that the truth of his discourse is that specific place which is the reverse side of his discourse, he devalues from the important to the fundamental. He then seeks a foundation for what he states in ideology (and this in all its forms) and elaborates a discourse on the world, forgetting that he is in the world.

When the lawyer becomes aware of the embarrassment of developing a programmatic discourse on the world, he can finally develop a discourse in the world and move from the fundamental to the important. A final trap then remains, since it is not possible to get out of language – truth being only a fall from the lawyer's knowledge into language itself – it is the ordinary language of his practice that he must question and abandon meaning and sign in favor of the ordinary signifiers he uses: there is, indeed, according to the famous formula, a whole mythology that is deposited in our language.

59 I. MURDOCH, *Sartre un rationaliste romantique*, Payot, Paris, 2015.

3 Is it still possible to criticise the Council of State?

For a logical examination of the validity of the administrative judge's "creations"

Since its origin, the administrative judge has been partly the creator of "administrative law": he regularly renews it on the basis of "definitions" of "concepts" or "notions," so many elements that seems necessary to him to carry out his office. In accordance with this contentious reality, he finds himself at a crossroads between a pragmatic legitimization linked to the realism of his mission and a legitimization induced by the respect of the formal validity of these decisions.

This duality manifests an ambivalence of validity understood according to a classical definition as existence (or as the counterpart of existence in the legal order).

Our aim will be to present a broader perception of validity in order to clarify this equivocation[1] which brings together a "decisionist" approach on the one hand[2,3] and a "normativist" approach on the other. The construction of a broad theory of validity should offer the capacity to perceive that validity must be understood as a combination of the judge's act of enunciation, the norm, and the enunciation itself. Validity is therefore different according to these three postures. Our intuition is that reducing validity to the purely formal (or syntactic) dimension of the norm creates a logical trap that prohibits criticism of the decision.

1 This ambivalence seems to lie in the fact that the opposition highlighted between "normativism" and "realism" must be strongly relativised. These two theoretical approaches are not the manifestation of a difference in "genus" but the manifestation of a difference between two "species" within the same genus. Professor Conte, in the above-mentioned text, has admirably demonstrated that normativism is, if one takes its logic to the extreme, based on judicial decisions "if the specific effectiveness within an ordering of a higher prescriptive proposition consists only in mediation which conditions the validity of lower prescriptive propositions, then the first and only prescriptive propositions which, in a legal system, no longer act as conditions for the validity of lower prescriptive propositions, but act on their own, are the lower prescriptive propositions: judicial decisions," (*op. cit.*, p. 723) and that the realism (which in his view should advantageously be presented as 'decisionalism') that Professor Conte divides into acritical realism and critical realism is presented in its critical form as a methodology of normativism – "critical decisionalism in fact proposes a method for verifying validity judgments relating to the prescriptive propositions" (*op. cit.*, p. 737) as a methodology of normativism.

2 "Realistic" in the legal sense of the term: justifying validity by its effects.

3 Justifying validity by its existence *in* and *by the* legal order according to a recursive definition of validity.

DOI: 10.4324/9781003130109-4

This clarification seems to us imperative today in order to be able to properly pass judgment – or develop a criticism in the noble sense of the term – with regard to the jurisprudence of the administrative court and in particular that of the Council of State. The remark could, of course, be developed for the benefit of other jurisdictions; nevertheless, the High Administrative Court offers a specific and particularly favorable field of analysis due to the jurisprudential nature of the development of administrative law and this in a cultural context dominated by *Civil Law*. Indeed, the aforementioned ambiguity implies either a forced adherence to what is stated as "positive law" itself, with the part of illusion that this tautology manifests, or a criticism that would be referred to an opposition of values, to a quarrel between value judgments on the basis or on the effectiveness of the proposed norm.

To clarify this ambiguity, we will therefore propose to extend the notion of validity in accordance with a semiotic and analytical approach to this term; then, we will attempt to justify the action of the administrative judge on the basis of its inclusion in the reality of litigation. We will see that what validates the action of the administrative judge is that the form of law lies in its very existence. That it reflects a certain truth of its enunciation and that the latter can be broken down in a logical way.

We shall therefore see in this study how the logical trap that renders certain criticisms futile manifests itself (I); then how it seems desirable to get out of it through the logical deconstruction inherent in the truth of the judge's discourse (II).

I The reduction of validity to formal validity: The construction of the logical trap

The jurisprudential creations of the administrative judge are legitimised either with reference to a "duty to be" and values or to the very "being" of the law. We will see that it is in the very logic of this legitimisation – which is similar to a "forced choice" – that these barriers are set up which prohibit criticism of the validity of the administrative judge's creations.

A The validity of the jurisprudential creations of the administrative judge by reference to the Sein and the Sollen

Traditionally, it is considered that the administrative judge plays a driving role in the elaboration of administrative law.[4] This function is fully manifested in his will – very

4 It is common to assert, following normative analyses, that the judge has the power to give concrete expression to the norm. Initially, the texts governing administrative law were imprecise and finally quite rare. In this sense, the normative function of the administrative judge is logically particularly developed. The main rules which thus concern "public liability," the "regime of administrative acts," were established on a jurisprudential basis. This approach is generally understood as making it possible to better adapt the function of the judge to changes in society; however, it is subject to two classic criticisms: the first concerns the questioning of "legal certainty" (*cf.* J. RIVERO, "Sur la rétroactivité de la règle jurisprudentielle," *AJDA*, 1968, p. 16); the second reflects the potentially embarrassing nature of a "moving" law which would be

regularly reaffirmed – to equip himself with the tools which appear to him as the most relevant in order to fulfil his role. The construction of "definitions,"[5] the elaboration of "concepts,"[6] or the implementation of "notions"[7] is almost like its "ordinary" function.[8] This situation is generally summed up supprimer the doctrine

(too) difficult to grasp in this respect. In fact, the role of the Council of State seems to go beyond this normative function: it increasingly plays the role of the intellectual body (Professor Caillosse, referring to Gramsci as the "organic intellectual") of the State through which it 'revives' the link between the State and the law. See J. CAILLOSSE, *L'État du droit administratif,* LGDJ, Paris, 2015, p. 300.

5 The Council of State has been led to produce certain definitions that are essential to its office, such as "public service," "public works," "public domain," etc. It should be noted that these definitions are always partly tautological (the equivalence between the *definidendum* and the *definiens: the* correct definition must be reciprocal) and that the definition itself consists, on the one hand, in determining *the intention of the* term and, on the other hand, in determining the extension of the term. With the definition it is a matter of fixing a term in a lexicon and thus making it possible to differentiate it on a synchronic basis from the other terms in the lexicon. The difference is then inherent in the language of specialisation being used.

6 Concepts must be understood as mental tools that allow a certain grasp of social reality. With a concept, it is a question, on the one hand, of answering a question inherent in the confrontation of a subject with this reality (it is, in this respect, that the relevance of the concepts is analysed). On the other hand, it is a question of normalising (concepts are normative) reality itself and thus expressing the fact that thinking is *normative*: by thinking about them we apply a norm to things. We always think about things in a certain way, starting from what matters most in terms of the relevance of the concept. The definition is the inscription of the concept in language and in a specific lexicon. In administrative law, concepts are essential: they express the singular way in which the judge apprehends the questions he considers important: they offer the means of establishing a relationship between the context in which a concept appears and the analysis of the truth of this concept. This truth being apprehended in a semantic sense as we shall see.

7 The notions are "conceptual envelopes" which seem to us to be marked by a vague and imprecise character. A kind of unthinking of the concept. The ordinary use of the term is particularly revealing here: the term vague is generally associated with the term notion. A precise notion would in this sense be an *oxymoron* and would denote, in fact, only a concept. In our lexicon we thus reject certain approaches that would make the notion the genus and the concept the species. There is, in our opinion, a difference in structure due to the use made of these terms. This is what the famous distinction between "conceptual notions" and "functional notions" by Dean Vedel (G. VEDEL, "De l'arrêt Septfonds à l'arrêt Barinstein (la légalité des actes administratifs devant les juridictions judiciaires), *JCP,* 1 (1948), p. 682). Likewise, on the basis of the difference in usage, Professor Tusseau's research: "Critique of a functional metanotion. La notion (trop) fonctionnelle de 'notion fonctionnelle'," *RFDA* (2009), p. 641. More broadly on these issues: G. TUSSEAU (ed.), *Les notions juridiques. Journée d'étude de la promotion d'agrégation de droit public,* Economica, Aix, Marseille, 2009 and J.P. BENOIT, "Notions et concepts, instruments of legal knowledge, Les leçons de la philosophie du droit de Hegel," in *Mélanges Peiser,* PUG, Paris, 1995, p. 27.

8 This concept of ordinariness seems essential to us because it is the ordinariness of a usage that gives a term its meaning (what is ordinary is the fact that we cannot think a thing other than by thinking it: that is, in the ordinary implementation of it in the world). This is a pragmatic definition that is illustrated by the consensus that is likely to be formed on the use of a word.

by the observation that administrative law is a praetorian law.[9] This French tradition of developing administrative law can be understood in various ways, but in our opinion it clearly demonstrates the inclusion within our legal tradition of a reflexive approach to the law which expresses a relatively marked form of legal realism.[10] According to this approach to litigation, the meaning of the regulation is discovered by an act of will of the judge and positive law is associated with the figure of legal operators and in particular with that of judges.[11]

This perfectly accepted approach – and one which seems to be just as perfectly assumed – deserves, however, to be analysed from a different angle than that usually accorded to it. Indeed, this question is regularly addressed from the aspect of the legitimacy of the judge (legitimacy to generate the rule of law) and has as its "background" the classic debate between "normativism" and "realism."[12]

The question can be analyzed as follows: the administrative judge on a praetorian basis regularly discovers new legal entities.[13] In this way, he manifests a

9 "[A]dministrative law is, in fact, much more than any other, dependent, due to the historical conditions of its development, on the work of the administrative judge and in particular of the Council of State, of which it should not be forgotten that it was, from the Cadot judgment … to the reform of the administrative jurisdiction brought about by the decrees of 30 September 1953, the ordinary law administrative judge," J.L. LACHAUME, *et al., Droit administratif: les grandes décisions de la jurisprudence*, 17th ed., PUF, Paris, 2017, p. 1.

10 Legal realism places the emphasis on the creative power of certain legal operators. The essential idea is to be "realistic" and to note that "positive law" is released by an act of will by legal operators. This realism is usually divided into two approaches which in certain aspects appear to be opposed: American realism and Scandinavian realism. American realism highlights the place and influence of the judge and sees him or her as involved in society (the risk is the inclusion of law in a certain sociology of law); Scandinavian realism, on the other hand, has focused on deconstructing meanings in accordance with the influence of the philosophy of language. Between these two approaches there is a somewhat moderate tendency expressed by Italian realism (a perfect illustration of which is provided by Professor Guastini) and contemporary French realism (which developed under the influence of Professor Troper and the Nanterre school), which is largely dependent on its transalpine counterpart.

11 For a critique of this reduction of legal operators to the figure of the judge: *cf.*, E. MILLARD, "Qui sont les opérateurs juridiques de R. Guastini," *Analisi e diritt* (2014), pp. 103–113.

12 On the limits of this opposition: *cf.* the classic study by Professor A.G. CONTE; "Primi argomenti per una critica del normativismo," in A.G. CONTE,*Filosofia del linguaggio normativo, III, studi 1995–2001,* Giappichelli, Torino, 2001, pp. 677–748. In this study, Professor de Pavia demonstrates that normativism logically carries a theory that seems to be irremediably opposed to it: decisionism (i.e., realism). Nor normativism through the concretisation of norms favours in the legal order: decisions. On this issue as well: A.G. CONTE, "In margine all'ultimo Kelsen," *Filosofia del linguaggio normativo, I, studi 1965–1981*, Giappichelli, Torino, 1981, pp. 17–30. For a French translation of the work of A.G. Conte, see P. RICHARD and A. PASSERINI-GLAZEL, eds, *Anthologie des textes du professeur A. G. Conte: recherches sur la philosophie du langage normatif*, to be published in 2021.

13 We will limit ourselves to mentioning only certain creations linked to what contemporary philosophy understands as social ontology: "the administrative contract"; "the interest to act"; "fundamental rights"; "general principles of law"; "objectives with constitutional values"; "the principle of legal security"; "the principle of solidarity."

creative power which expresses a certain relationship with regard to the "legal norm."[14] This is generally deduced from the presence of an (internal or external) text which is interpreted by an act of will.[15] It also happens that the judge detaches himself from this requirement of a text in order to focus on the interpretation of a social situation.[16] Naturally, this action is often masked by a certain voluntary confusion between causes and reasons.[17] In the argumentation which is specific to the justification of these creations, it is thus suggested that this jurisprudential activity is *causally* generated by certain elements whereas these are only the reasons inherent in the decision and therefore not *a priori justifying* elements, but a *rational* justification *a posteriori*. This, of course, is not absolute and there are constraints which are either "referential"[18] (for example, the plurality of interpreters and the actual relations between legal systems) or "inferential"[19]

14 This term is in itself ambiguous and deserves to be clarified: beyond the metonymy that sometimes plays between the standard and its vehicle, different conceptions of the standard are possible: the standard can be presented as a "deontic statement" (this is the purpose of the above-mentioned metonymy), a "deontic proposition" (N. Bobbio), "deontic enunciation" (G. Ledig), "deontic status" or a "deontic noème" (A.G. Conte), a "mental tool" (P. Amselek).

15 On this question: P. BRUNET, "Les juges européens au pays des valeurs," in *La vie des idées*, June, 2009.

16 See the following classic studies: R. CHAPUS, "De la valeur juridique des principes généraux du droit et des autres règles jurisprudentielles du droit administratif," *Dalloz*, 1966, p. 99; J.P. CHAUDET, "Les principes généraux de la procédure administrative contentieuse, *LGDJ*, 1967; J. RIVERO, "Le juge administratif français: un juge qui gouverne?" *Dalloz*, 1951, p. 23. It should be noted that the term "general rule of procedure" seems to have disappeared in favour of "general principles of law." Professor Chapus could observe in his manual *Droit du contentieux administratif*, 20th ed. Domat droit public, Montchrestien, p. 103: "the general rules of procedure … apply in the silence of texts." Naturally, as the aforementioned "moderate" realistic doctrine notes, the judge's intervention does not take place in a vacuum: the decision will generally be taken in a field which has already been the subject of cognitive work by the doctrine or by other courts which have already worked on the concept. In this sense, the judge will have the option of either deciding on a completely new solution (but in this case he will not be able to use a justification argument in the cognitive work carried out by the other legal operators) or choosing his solution from the list of solutions that are previously stated by the various legal operators (in the latter case his power is no longer arbitrary but discretionary).

17 On this inversion regularly presents *cf.* J. Bouveresse's research, for example: J. BOUVERESSE, *Wittgenstein: La rime et la raison, science éthique et esthétique*," Les éditions de minuit, Paris, 1973. In particular Chapter 5: "Causes, reasons and myths": "it is not because phenomena have a hidden meaning that we can interpret them, it is because we interpret them that they have a hidden meaning," p. 211.

18 The logic of denotation or reference implies the presence of constraints that are real. On this question it would be useful to cross-reference this analysis with the theory of legal constraints as envisaged by the Nanterre school.

19 There are also constraints that manifest themselves as inferential, as R. Brandom seeks to demonstrate. *Cf.* to cite just one work that presents itself as a synthesis of his thought: R. BRANDOM, *L'articulation des raisons: Introduction à l'inférentialisme*," Cerf, Paris, 2009.

(through a kind of "conceptual holism"[20] which means that when I mobilise a concept I will necessarily mobilise all those who are connected with it).

B The aporia of validity by the Sollen*: Behind the ideological claim to the* Sollen*, the logical relationship to the* Breast

This situation seems to be able to be legitimised, in accordance with this realistic approach of the administrative judge, in relation to a certain *Sollen* (on the apparent paradox *cf.* the logical weakening of the distinction between realism and normativism). The judge can thus by an act of will generate a normative state of affairs: the judge justifies this creation by its conformity to shared values.[21] There would thus be an intentionality on the part of the judge oriented in accordance with the search for certain social values or for the benefit of certain choices in society. His case law would be nothing more than the expression of values.

There is here an approximation of the legal order as generated by the administrative judge with a "duty to be" (on the basis that the judge generates the law, because it clarifies the meaning of the regulation, there will in a supprimer way not be a normative pyramid which would be prior, but a hierarchy of standards generated by the action of the judge with, as shown by case law, a mobile axiological hierarchy, because it is subject to weighting which is carried out on a case-by-case basis). This justification by the *Sollen is* clearly ideological. As such, it appears undecidable: how to indeed, make a "rational" choice between different ideologies and between different paradigms? The choice will be an arbitrary one, reflecting the freedom of the interpreter, since rationality is only constructed within a paradigm and never between two paradigms. Moreover – and in a purely logical way – we know that just because something "must be" does not mean that it "is."[22] This is a delicate leap to make, especially from the perspective of the equivalence between validity and existence.

20 It is clear that the use of a concept infers in a space of exchange the mastery of all the concepts that are associated with the one that is mobilized in an argumentation. In this sense, it is soon the whole language that is mobilised in this exchange. The constraint is therefore to master the use of these elements and their articulation. For Brandom, inferential semantics is necessarily holistic: "one cannot have concepts at all unless one has many concepts." *See* R. BRANDOM, *L'articulation des raisons, op. cit.* p. 23. In the end, Bourdieu was saying no other thing: "(it is because of the fact that lawyers) have a capital of words, a capital of concepts that they can contribute to the construction of reality," P. BOURDIEU, *Sur l'État, course at the Collège de France, 1989–1992,* Seuil, Paris, 1992, p. 523.

21 In the field of the affirmation of "principles" or "general principles of law," this position is obvious: "the general principles of law therefore appear as jurisprudential norms created by the judge – usually administrative, but also, if necessary, by the Court of Cassation or the Constitutional Council – from the ideological conceptions of the national conscience and/or from a mass of constitutional, international or legislative texts": *cf.* P.-L. FRIER and J. PETIT, *Droit administratif,* 10 ed., LGDJ, Paris, p. 111.

22 In accordance with Hume's Law.

The administrative norm discovered by the judge would thus be valid within the administrative order by reference to the validity of the latter and as it is elaborated from its actual value.[23] Here we have a pragmatist who is rooted in a value judgment on the action of the administrative judge with regard to the society but who manifests a circular reasoning.

The "jurisprudential policy" of the administrative judge would thus only be "policy" and "policy of values"?[24] This response seems particularly dangerous to us, because it is then difficult for the doctrine to criticise the action of the administrative judge – the risk, in fact, is: either to be opposed to a "confit of values"[25] or to lock oneself into a purely formal criticism in which, in the end, the basis of positive law is the judicial decision. In so doing, such an approach seems to us to prevent the doctrine – as a discourse on law – from playing its descriptive and non-prescriptive role. It is then imperative to find other sources of justification for the creative action of the judge and the validity of that action. To achieve this goal, we need to clarify what we mean by validity.

23 On this evolution of the law and in particular of administrative law: P. MOOR, *Dynamique du système juridique: Une théorie générale du droit,* Bruylant, LGDJ, Paris, 2010, pp. 135–162. On administrative law: *Droit administratif,* vol. 1 and 2, Stampfli, Bern, 3rd ed. for volume 1 with A. Fluckiger and V. Martenet, 2012; and for volume 2 with E. Poltier, 2011; *Permeability of the Legal System: Essays on the Rule of Law,* PUL, Paris, 2016. Administrative law according to P. Moor has been the subject of three "moments" that were articulated and appeared to be "mutually necessary." A "police administrative law" has been replaced by a "management administrative law" and the latter is now giving way to a "redistribution administrative law." The purpose of the latter is to take account of new interests – a kind of redistribution of the "commons": the environment, education, energy. Traditionally, this right was more the right of the state than the affirmation of the rule of law and was manifested in a political form. Its rationale was not simply to stabilise normative expectations of behaviour, but to provide legitimacy to legal discourse through legislation. This paradigm is currently in crisis and the political dimension of legitimacy is being challenged by the economic subsystem. Public interests no longer develop in parallel and are no longer ranked in a hierarchy under the legitimacy of politics, but overlap and offer themselves to a logic of weighting; the universality and precision of the norm give way to taking into account "the ground" and to implementation, leading to an inversion of the pyramid of norms by making them concrete; rules retreat in the face of the empire of principles.

24 A source of the validity of norms understood as specific existence is to be found in the philosophy of Rudolph Hermann Lotze, in neo-Kantism and in the philosophy of values (especially in Heinrich Rickert, Wilheim Windelband, Bruno Bauch, Emil Lask), in axiology (for which I refer to the most eminent representative of contemporary philosophy, Robert Schirokauer Hartman).

25 This approach explains the use of the balancing of principles technique in the context of administrative litigation. It should be noted that this is ultimately a transposition of the distinction between rules and principles if the rules imply an acceptance or rejection of the normative proposal that they convey the principles would, for their part, carry a weight that would have to be weighed when the principle is opposed to another principle. Naturally, this technique of frequent use is of ultimate benefit to the judge: it gives them even greater scope for creating law.

II The development from formal validity to semantic validity and pragmatic validity: Logic as a way out of the trap

To get out of this logical trap, it is necessary to perceive that the form of law is to be found in the specific modalities of its "existence." These are manifested in the form of validity according to three species that cannot be reduced to a single genus. Validity thus expresses three dimensions of the being of law: its enunciations (deontic acts), its statements (deontic phrases), and its propositions (deontic states of affairs). Through these three dimensions, supprimer law forms reality and therefore engenders a specific relationship with the truth it enunciates. Traditionally, only semantic validity, that which derives from syntagms, is presented as assimilable or the *analogon of* classical truth. However, this truth is perfectly recursive and does not "in itself" offer a way out of the logical trap we have uncovered. It will therefore be necessary to consider other answers. The most relevant one seems supprimer to lie in the idea that the form of the law that underpins its existence is the very being of the act of enunciation, which is likely to give substance to the truth of the creation of case law: this creation manifests (or not) an agreement not on a concept, but on criteria logically prior to it.

A The logical plurality of the concept of validity

It is therefore necessary, beforehand, to have a clear vision of this legal concept.[26] Validity seems to be expressed in the following way:[27] it can be either "formal," "material," or "axiological."[28] It is understandable that validity in the "legally traditional" sense of the term manifests itself with "formal validity." There is thus an opposition between a validity that is understood on the basis of its causes (values: axiological validity) or its effects (effectiveness: material validity) and a validity that is taken seriously for what it "is"; the existence of the norm in the order of law (formal validity). This (existence) is not then an attribute of validity, but happens to be validity itself. However, this formal validity logically closes in on the norm that gives concrete expression to it in the judicial decision.

26 Validity is the modality of existence of the norm in the order of law according to Kelsen's famous formula. The equivalence between validity and existence is set out in *Recht und Logic of* 1965. He observes the validated is the existence is the specific existence of prescriptive propositions. On this question *cf.* the aforementioned text by Professor Conte, who conducts a close study of this question: A.G. CONTE, "In margine dell'ultimo Kelsen," *op. cit.*

27 It is also necessary to distinguish between the validity of *the* legal order and validity *within* the legal order: the two elements are naturally linked.

28 On these distinctions: A.G. CONTE, "Minima deontica", *filosofia del linguaggio normatico, II, op. cit.* pp. 357–407. Also the entry 'validity' in *Novissimo Digesto italiano,* UTET, Torino, 20 (1975), pp. 418–425. In this point 3, we rely on the analyses of the concept of validity in these different dimensions on the analyses carried out by Professor Conte, which appear to us to be the reference with regard to the logical analysis of the different implications of the concept.

As Professor Conte has demonstrated – in our opinion definitively – this, however classic, approach to validity in the form of three "species" belonging to the same "genus" gives rise to an embarrassing illusion. In fact, we are talking about three different "genera" and not three "species" of the same genus. In fact, these three approaches to validity are quite clearly predefined by different objects. For example, if, from a normative statement, it is possible to implement an analysis according to the terms of "formal validity," it will be impossible to carry out an analysis according to the terms of "axiological validity" on the same premises. In this sense, clearly, the three approaches reflect three different 'genres' that need to be distinguished: there is what Professor Conte presents as a "syntagmatic," "semantic" and "pragmatic" approach to validity.

This theoretical approach seems supprimer to be of extreme interest, not only from the theoretical perspective of the construction of a phenomenology of validity, but also and perhaps above all in order to clarify the various manifestations of the judge's action in his discovery of new legal entities. Validity as it is usually taken as an argument to legitimise in positive law the existence of a norm takes the form of formal validity. This approach to validity appears as syntagmatic. It is this approach which is used as an argument by the administrative court. It would indeed be surprising in view of his necessary search for legitimacy if the judge were to state "openly" that he decides on the basis of values or the recognition of the effectiveness of various rules already present in a society – even if this is often what he seems to do beyond the classical judicial rhetoric.[29]

The judge's official line of argument therefore lies in his or her desire to be anchored in syntactic validity, whereas very often – *de facto* – what is achieved is either a reference to an act (free not nature) or an express reference to a linguistic statement that supports a norm (by nature without prior meaning). The formal and syntactic dimension thus offers to mask the pragmatic and semantic aspects of the action of the administrative judge. This is a kind of voluntary denial, with regard to reality, of[30] his action in favor of the form of law.[31] When the judge, through a "deontic act of language," creates a "legal status" (a legal or deontic "state of affairs"), he implements a validity that is pragmatic, and when he discovers the meaning of a linguistic statement by linking it to what exists in the world, he carries out a semantic action that can only be apprehended through an approach to validity that is itself semantic.

Formal or syntactic validity, on the other hand, is concerned only with the analysis of legal *status* (which is generated by deontic performative acts) within the legal order.

29 The need to find a textual reference to his creations is becoming more and more of an argumentative constraint.

30 The semantic conception of semantic truth that we seek to distinguish from a semantic truth that would be understood as *consensus* (a pragmatic conception of semantic truth) or as *coherence* (a syntactic conception of semantic truth).

31 Embarrassment seems to be manifested here in the oblivion of the fact that the specific form of the right is its existence.

Let us clarify things the administrative judge carries out acts of speech which generate deontic statuses which are subject to an examination proper to formal (syntactic) validity and which can be assessed semantically on the basis of a relationship between the deontic statement and the reality of the deontic status.

This clarification is necessary, because what in the dominant discourse justifies the action of the administrative judge in his creative work – which is generally recognised as a quality by the various commentators – is the realism of a judge who "judges the administration" knows the administration and its needs and therefore appears to be endowed with great pragmatism and realism with regard to his mission. What legitimises his role is therefore his capacity to generate relevant "action patterns" and "interpretation patterns." It is his capacity to be in the world and to act on it. What validates the creative action of the administrative judge is the fact that he is able to make the action possible or intelligible and that he offers certain valid explanations to the world of administration. In a way, we find here Professor Amselek's famous distinction between the norm as an instrument for measuring the possible and the command (what is put in the hand so that he who is endowed with the thing can lend an ear to what it evokes as a measure).

The entities generated by the administrative judge must, therefore, conform in some way to the reality in which they must play: this is the basis of the relevance of the conceptual creation of the administrative judge.

The example of the construction of the decisive act. Let us take an example in order to give an account of the various dimensions of this complex approach to validity: when the administrative court seeks to characterise the existence of a decisive act.[32] The court will develop this "concept" by making use of its "extension." He thus considers that the decisive act is an individual act and that it has a decisive character which is manifested in the fact that the will of the administration is likely to bring about a modification in the legal order. The conceptual envelope, as always, is in our example singled out by two dimensions: the "understanding" of the concept (the attributes of the concept) and the "extension" of the concept (the acts that are likely to be included in this conceptual envelope and this in accordance with the understanding of the concept). These two dimensions are inversely proportional: the more understanding is developed the less extension is strong and the less understanding is developed the greater the extension. When the judge decides, in the course of case law, to refine the definition of the concept, he carries out several simultaneous actions which present themselves as pragmatic, syntactic and semantic.

The enunciation of the court decision, itself, which decides to reduce or develop the concept is an act.[33] More precisely, it is an act that gives rise to the presence of a legal status (state of affairs). If, for example, the Council of State

32 In J. MORANT-DEVILLER, P. BOURDON, P. BOURDON and F. POULET, *Droit administratif*, 15th ed., LGDJ, Paris, 2017, p. 392, "La décision administrative donnant à l'administration le privilège du préalable règle fondamentale du droit public est au sein des actes unilatéraux une décision qui modifie l'ordre juridique existant, confère des droits aux particuliers ou mettre des obligations à leur charge."

33 It is an act of producing a statement. The enunciation as an act of linguistic production is opposed within the framework of linguistics to the utterance that is the result of this

considers that the administration's formal notices do not constitute a decision when they are merely invitations and that it is different when they are accompanied by sanctions or when they set a time limit within which the person concerned must comply with what is expected from him (*cf.* CE, January 25, 1991, *Confédération nationale des associations familiales catholiques*), it produces a deontic *status*. It produces a legal status. The validity of this act can logically only be assessed in terms of its pragmatic validity. The act must necessarily conform to its concept or it must conform to a possible hypothetico-constitutive norm.

For example, it is inherent in the very concept of a court decision to decide a dispute as it is inherent in the concept of a promise not to be promised for the past, etc. What the act generates is a *status* that will be set by the statement. Syntactic (or formal) validity will then take over. Statements can be deontic, proclamatory or declarative. The statement *sets out* a "normative state of affairs" which must be valid in the formal sense of the term. It will therefore be necessary to find a higher standard that validates the existence of the statement and the proposal it supports. It will thus be necessary to find standards of empowerment that provide the judge and the administration with the framework of its power. It will then be necessary to refer to the texts that concern, for example, circulars or directives, etc.[34] Similarly, it will be necessary to refer to the texts that define the office of the judge.[35] It is at this level where the idea, that the existence of the norm is *in* and *through the* legal system, is fully in play in accordance with a definition of validity that is largely recursive.

B The tautology expressed by semantic validity

The claimed inclusion of the realistic and pragmatic function of the judge in the world is regularly manifested by the assertion that the judge reports and elaborates the "judicial truth." The latter emerges from a certain perception of semantic validity of which it is the analogon. Semantic validity is therefore only the truth of the deontic statement. Traditionally, this truth of the statement in conformity with the denotation is understood to be an account of the presence of an object of the world (the word cat, for example, denotes an animal, etc.).

For example: the statement "monumental perspective" refers to or denotes a certain avenue with a certain quality of view.[36] This classic approach to denotation is, however, difficult to implement in law and in particular administrative law, because legal concepts often generate the reality they refer to. This is demonstrated

production. In this sense, enunciation can appear as the actualization of sentences in a specific situation.

34 On these issues: B. DEFOORT, *La décision administrative*, LGDJ, Paris, 2015; G. KOUBI, *Les circulaires administratives*, Economica, Paris, 2003.

35 See, *Code of Administrative Procedure, Code of Relations between the Public and the Administration*, Lexis Nexis, 2018, 2nd ed.

36 Naturally, the trap would be to believe that it is the thing itself that the judge is going to grasp in his work of legal qualification, but it is the thing in so far as it is grasped within a certain theme, as we shall see later.

by the work inherent in what is presented as relating to social ontology. Moreover, even beyond this lack of denotation, some authors believe that it is not possible to determine the "truth" of prescriptive statements.[37] Rebuttal is possible, but it requires either acceptance of the idea of a deontic reality or a tautological definition of the denotation.

It seems desirable supprimer to answer these two questions by noting, on the one hand, that the object of the denotation is (in a contemporary perception of semantic truth) another language different from that of the statement whose truth supprimer (in this sense, the truth in law is not *to re,* but of *dicto)* and, on the other hand, that the performative enunciation of a prescriptive deontic statement theoretically produces (it sets) the deontic status expressed by the prescriptive deontic statement and thereby engenders *the dicto* truth of that statement. In Professor Passerini's words, true norms are thus true norms. This truth is therefore tautological. In doing so, we certainly have the possibility of envisaging this semantic truth, but since it is recursive, it will offer us nothing but a tautology: absolutely true, but empty of knowledge. This semantic approach to the truth does not therefore seem likely to legitimise the action of the administrative judge.

*C Use of **pragmatic validity***

What this analysis of "semantic validity" shows is that the law participates in the creation of what it deals with. In this sense, the relationship to truth, perhaps the most relevant one, must be sought in a philosophical realism supprimer concerned, without metaphysics, with thinking properly about its relationship to reality (i.e., its elaborate character) and objectivity (thereby challenging a certain relativism). If the form of law lies in its "being" and in its "existence," we must accept the idea that it is in itself the norm of the reality it generates. With regard to objectivity, it is presented in the acceptance of the idea that one can only think what one is "capable" of thinking. Here, I mean the fact that I only think in a given situation – which is the 'format' of my thinking. If thought does not access the thing, but generates it, then it is not possible for me to think about the thing

37 As Prof. L. Passerini Glazel demonstrates it is possible following the work of Prof. A.G. Conte to distinguish the following situation: two concepts of the true manifest themselves (truth of *dicto* and truth of *re*). The truth of *dicto* is that which is predicated on statements, whereas the truth of *re* is predicated on things. The widespread thesis that norms cannot be regarded as true or false is based on the *dicto truth* of norms. This thesis is, however, denied by Kalinowski and Conte. For Kalinowki there is a deontic reality that exists before norms. Conte's analysis, for its part, is not based on the existence of such a deontic reality: according to him, norms are statements that verify themselves on the basis of a kind of retroactive performativity. The performative enunciation of a prescriptive deontic statement theoretically produces (it poses) the deontic status expressed by the prescriptive deontic statement and thereby engenders the *dicto* truth of this statement. *Cf.* A. PASSERINI GLAZEL, *Atto, norma, tipo: tra pragmatica e ontologia del diritto*, Aracne, Rome, 2012 and more specifically "norme vere, vere norme," pp. 211–219.

without this architecture of thoughts.[38] This reality is objective even if the formats may be relative.[39]

In the judge's invention within the litigation area, two aspects are apparent: the meaning of his decision, which is the specific way in which he is going to deal with the problem, and the meaning of the decision (what it denotes), which is presented as the specific format in which the problem appeared to be important. In and through the "meaning" of a decision something is attained that stands beyond thought: the "significance" of the decision. The "meaning" of a provision – discovered or invented by the judge – would thus be its intentional aim. supprimer the particular way in which the legal operator is led to think about the legal relationship in a given situation with the aim of arriving at a decision. In accordance with this analysis, denotation (unlike meaning) could be presented not as an object of the world that the norm is going to establish as a state of affairs, but as the frame of reference in which the question is raised: its singular horizon of appearance and enunciation.

The norm expressed by the judge manifests this reality discovered by the philosophy that thought, expressed through language, does not access any "true" reality, but rather norms are in reality what counts in a given context and allows us to orient ourselves and measure what it is possible to do. I cannot think that the thing "as it is" is thought.[40] The judge in his normative activity reactivates the idea that each situation implies its own measure and therefore its own standard capable of grasping what is important; that is what counts in this situation.

The format is the way in which the creation of jurisprudence will be thematised: this thematisation is achieved by agreeing on the *criteria of what* is important.

In the context of litigation, we in fact show only peripheral or marginal disagreements on the criteria of this law.[41] The conceptual evolutions and reversals of case law and the creations inherent in them express this pre-eminence of the *criterion* over the *concept.* Disagreement on the criteria offers the possibility of questioning the relevance of the concept.

It should be noted that the criteria do not so much allow us to be certain about the reality of a thing as to identify what that thing is in order to better "find our way."

38 *Cf.* on these questions the very rich reflection developed on the concept of constitutive norms, both in the framework of classical philosophy since Kant, Wittgenstein and Wittgenstein and in the field of law: Johannes Thomae (1840–1921); Edmund Husserl (1859–1938); Max Weber (1864–1920); Ferdinand de Saussure (1857–1913); Ernst Mally (1879–1944), the first of the inventors of *deontisch* and *Deontik;* Hans Kelsen (1881–1873): Czeslaw Zna Mierowski (1888–1967); Ludwig Wittgenstein (1889–1951); Antonino Pagliaro (1898–1967); Alf Ross (1899–1979); John von Neumann (1903 1957) and Oskar Morgenstern (1902–1977); Max Black (1909–1988); Georg Henrik von Wright (1916–2003); John Rawls (1921–2002).

39 It is obvious that truth presupposes reality but reality does not presuppose truth.

40 On these issues: J. BENOIST, *L'adresse du réel,* Vrin, Paris, 2017.

41 As Wittgenstein puts it: "We judge an action by its background in human life.... The background is the train of life," WITTGENSTEIN L. (1980), *Bemerkungen über die Philosophie der Psychologie*, Vols I and II, G.E.M. Anscombe and G.H. von Wright, eds, Blackwell, Oxford. §§ 624–625.

By using criteria, we are not trying to explain, or *prove* the fact that we have agreed among ourselves in words (and therefore in life forms). We only describes the same fact in another way; or rather, there is a possible recourse when agreement is threatened, or lost. We use official criteria when value judgements have to be made; but we use the criteria as understood by Wittgenstein when "we don't know where we stand," when we are lost in relation to our words, and the world they anticipate. We then seek to find ourselves again by discovering and declaring the criteria on which we agree.[42] the attention paid to the ordinary of litigation would be able to reveal what the everyday life of litigation conceals: it is the manifestation of a skeptical tendency (in the sense of American philosophy) specific to language, which implies that, with the everyday use of language, there is a power of repudiation of its capacity to tell the world "as it is."

In this sense, who has never been so surprised by rediscovering the strange heuristic capacity of an etymology for the benefit of their understanding of the world? Law as a language of specialization perfectly expresses this linguistic reality: the "constitutive rules," for example, clearly express this occultation. The law would be, through the latter, capable of engendering the reality to which it relates. However, even with these so-called constitutive rules, the ontological support of what is instituted remains always present – and more or less decisive. Thus, to take just one example, even an almost self-referential system such as a game (e.g., chess) must assume an object capable of taking on the role engendered by the constitutive rule. Rules, by their very nature (by grammatical necessity), must be followed in the world, and in relation to them there is a scale of influence of the ontological support of the norm which means that certain rules (those supprimer said to be technical or regulatory) are strongly influenced by the ontological support, whereas the so-called constitutive rules have a leaner ontological support. Each time, however, the link with the world and with a certain form of life in which the law and the rules are implemented becomes apparent: how could it be otherwise.

For legal operators with litigation, it is thus a question of criticizing agreements, rules … and finally, mainly the "concepts" which until now have made it possible to confirm – or reassure – our agreement in legal language. It is the coherence of the concepts and the preliminary criteria on which we agree that often remains ordinarily invisible.

Sometimes this agreement, due to the tautological nature of positive law, needs to be reinterpreted and this action of renegotiation can only take place within the adopted conceptual scheme. What is therefore under consideration in the context of the litigation is the difficulty inherent in our genuine participation in this

42 S. CAVELL (1979), *The Claim of Reason*, Oxford University Press, New York, 1979, p. 71. For a typically legal analysis of this difference between the ontological weight of constitutive and regulative norms: W. ELANIEC, 'Sull'idea stessa di regola costitutiva', in *Ontologia sociale, Potere deontico e regole costitutivo,* P. DI LUCIA (ed.), Quodlibet, Macerata, 2003, pp. 155–179. This analysis is of particular importance for administrative law and its contemporary developments as put into perspective in note 24. This approach offers an analytical grid which seems to us to be relevant to the implementation of the technical standards that proliferate within administrative law.

"conversation of justice"[43] and yet essential with regard to our social agreement as[44] perfectly analysed by Cavell on the basis of Rawls' work.[45] It is understandable that the validity and effectiveness of positive law lies in this pragmatic dimension and in the possibility for the law to repeat its reality in this way tirelessly.

All in all, what the clarification of validity and reflection on the possibility of developing a critique of the judge's role shows us, is that the ordinary of a "life form" always takes precedence over legal reasoning. If a decision leads to discussion and the latter develops, it is often because the "scheme," the "format," the "theme" chosen by the judge, and the "concept," the "meaning," the "cognitive hold," which is on this basis realised by the judge is a violence made by the judge not to reality, but to the form of life in which he participates and at the heart of which he is supposed to place his deontic enunciation. Finally, it is that the pragmatic act likely to generate a legal status through the thetical nature of the utterance is invalid either with regard to the concept it develops or to the hypothetico-constitutive norm that should legitimise its action.

Can be disappointed with such a conclusion with regard to the apparatus mobilised to achieve it and some will say that this is only "common sense,"[46] but it is still necessary to make good use of it, which is the challenge of pragmatic validity.

43 On this question: S. CAVELL, "La conversation de la justice: Rawls et le théâtre du consentement," in *Qu'est-ce que la philosophie américaine*, Gallimard, Paris, p. 369.

44 On this issue the important work of S. LAUGIER based on the work of S. Cavell on conversation and democracy. We will limit ourselves to quoting Chapter IV of the work *Recommencer la philosophie: Stanley Cavell et la philosophie en Amérique*, Vrin, Paris, 2014, pp. 147–178. Also D. LORENZINI, *Éthique et politique de soi; Foucault, Hadot, Cavell et les techniques de l'ordinaire*, Vrin, Paris, 2015.

45 S. CAVELL, "The Conversation of Justice," *op. cit.* The idea that emerges is the one that will be taken up again later in the study of remarriage comedies. "This projects the idea that what constitutes a marriage is not to be found, so to speak, outside marriage (in the Church, the State, sexual satisfaction, or the promise of offspring) but in the readiness to repeat the recognition of its reality, as if every genuine marriage were a remarriage." *Op. cit.*, p. 374.

46 "Common sense is the best shared thing, because everyone thinks they are so well provided for, that even those who are the most difficult to satisfy in anything else are not accustomed to wanting more than they have. In what way it is not probable that all are mistaken; but rather it testifies that the power to judge well, and to distinguish the true from the false, which is properly what is called common sense or reason, is naturally equal in every man; and that thus the diversity of our opinions does not come from the fact that some are more reasonable than others, but only from the fact that we conduct our thoughts in different ways, and do not consider the same things. For it is not enough to have a good mind, but the main thing is to apply it well."

4 The meaning of the fault "as such ..."

The various studies[1] which vary the concepts of fault (and its linguistic translation) in time and space seem to indicate the emergence of a "conceptual knot" or "family resemblance."[2]

From this perspective, fault is usually understood in two ways: either as the predicate of a subject, or as the subject of a judgment. In this presentation, we perceive the classical opposition between analytical judgments and synthetic judgments.[3]

We also discern the presence of a question that could be expressed in the following form: Can the fault be apprehended from the analysis of its concept or can it be appreciated from an empirical situation – from a state of affairs expressed in a synthetic form?

1 On the presence of this conceptual knot: A.G. CONTE, "Il linguaggio della colpa e del peccato: colpa peccato verità," in *Filosofia del linguaggio normativo*, Giappichelli, Torino, 2001, pp. 989–1000. The author of this text states as follows: "There is a conceptual knot between the three concepts of fault, debt and duty. This is confirmed by a second nodosity which is manifested, for its part, between the names given to these three concepts."

2 "Family resemblance" can be linked in various ways (as demonstrated by certain linguistic evidence): these links appear between *colpa* (fault, guilt) and *dovere*; between *colpa* and *debito* (duty); and between *dovere* and *debito* (debt). Between *colpa* and *dovere*: this relationship exists in the Polish language (*wina*: links with *dovere, obbligo, Pflicht, duty*]; in the German language (*Schuld* which means either *colpa* or *debito* and which etymologically is close to *sollen* or *shall*); between *colpa* and *debito*: in Polish (*byc winnym*: guilty; *byc diuznym*: indebted, debt); but also in German (*Schuld* can be presented as having the meaning *guilt*, *guilt*, but also *debito*, debt, *debt*); and in Danish (*skyld: culpa, guilt, guilt; gaeld: debito*, debt, *debt*).

The "family resemblance" naturally refers to the concept of § 67 of the *Recherches philosophiques* by L. Wittgenstein. "I cannot better characterise these analogies than by the word: 'family resemblance'; for it is in this way that the different resemblances that exist between the different members of a family intertwine and wrap around each other: height, facial features, eye color, gait, temperament, etc., and that is how the family resembles each other."

3 For example: "The State is at fault," "Mr. X committed a fault"; "Intentional fault," "simple fault" etc.

DOI: 10.4324/9781003130109-5

It is to clarify this nodosity that we have been working on. It was a question of trying to respond to the problem posed by the diversity of enunciations[4] (and uses) with regard to the unity (or identity) of the meanings to which reason seems to bring us back to.[5,6] In this sense, "to speak of fault" is apparently to enter into a particular relationship with the world and this by means of a specific "doing" that implies our consciousness and our intentionality. The capacity offered to men to state certain things does not consist in keeping away from the world (or to state things about it), but is presented as an activity of the world. It is a question of working in the world in this way.

In accordance with this orientation, we have opted for a phenomenological approach that combines the analysis of the legal language as it is used, and the possible ante-predatory elements that could be supported by this language. Naturally, it is not a question of yielding to a magical conception of the real, but of taking note of the fact that the real is elaborated by language, and this in the world. The fault will thus be apprehended from a synthesis of the relations among a legal entity, a legal act, and a norm.

Our wager was, therefore, to answer three questions:

1 Is the "meaning of fault" in the legal field linked more to a way of "speaking" (language games, "uses," etc.) than to a way of "thinking" (a logical necessity or a material *a priori*)[7]?
2 Should the "meaning of the fault" then be the object of a particular intuition in order to offer knowledge: a theme?
3 Finally, does the "meaning of the fault" manifest the presence not of a particular "essence," but of a "nature" that can be thematised?

We will thus have to distinguish the object that is targeted with the fault and understand how to add to its specific intentional modality[8] that will give it not only a meaning, but also a *meaning.*[9]

4 Are etymologically close: in Italian *dovere* and *debito*; in French devoir et dette; in Portuguese *dever* and *divida*; in Castilian *deber* and *deuda*. These terms derive from the Latin verb *debeo*. On all these issues see A.G. CONTE, "*Il linguaggio...*" *op. cit.*
5 How to speak properly with words and in particular with the one that gives the meaning
6 Fact, we can see that the same object can give rise to expressions that do not have the same meaning.
7 GARDIES, *Essai sur les fondements a priori de la rationalité morale et juridique*, LGDJ, Paris, 1972.
8 In the phenomenological conception, intentionality should be understood in the following way: it presents itself as a structural characteristic of consciousness. The experiences of consciousness must therefore be understood as the aim of an object that remains transcendent to it. The intentional act is thus correlated to an object "as" it is thus aimed at by the consciousness. One understands, in this way, to what extent this concept is intimately linked to phenomenology. We will see that this object will be founded, according to a particular register (as a categorical objectivity) and not as a real object.
9 This reflection is essentially epistemological in its approach.

1 *Talking about* the fault or *thinking about* the fault

Since Kant, it is common to consider that any structuring of experience is extrinsic to it. After "the wall of the transcendental," there also appears "a wall of silence" that is just as difficult to overturn. In this sense, the law would "silence" not only "the thing in itself" that it seeks to treat but also the structure of its own experience. The "concept of fault," thus caught in the nets of language, would necessarily fail to encounter "the fault *itself*" and to experience its own meaning. Legal meaning would mask the grammatical structure as well as the normative choices that are made on these bases. It is finally an opposition between a priority given to an *a priori* concept (fault being an ideal concept, it does not refer to anything physical) or a mediation of this concept by the norm that must be faced (thus, finally, a regulated use of language by its uses): either the concept is created by the norm, or it is discovered by the norm.[10]

This opposition is made complex by the fact that meaning is inherent in thinking (as intentionality and as denotation) and speech (as part of the construction of meaning). Thinking and speaking are thus, in a way, mutually supportive.

When legal systems incorporate the "concept of fault," it is therefore a certain relationship to the world supprimer they seem to be based on. This relationship would be linked to an initial choice: it may, on the one hand, seek to construct a kind of correlation between the world and language (which thus seeks to describe or understand it); it may, on the other hand, be inherent in the very structure of language and, *in fine*, to "grammatical" constraints. In this way, an approach according to which intentionality is oriented towards the world and an approach according to which intention is included in language and its rules are opposed.[11]

Let's clarify what we mean by "concept" and "conceptual." A concept aims to offer to the user a capacity to discriminate within a situation and this from certain normative choices. The "concept of fault" would, therefore, make it possible to account for a category of situations and to guide actions in the face of these

10 On this question: L. PASSERINI GLAZEL, "Eidologique et eidonomique dans la philosophie de l'acte juridique: Adolf Reinach et Czeslaw Znamierowski," in J. BENOIST and J.-F. KERVEGAN, eds, *Adolf Reinach entre droit et phénoménologie*, CNRS, Paris, 2008, pp. 59–70. Also by the same author, *Atto norma tipo*, ed. Aracne, Roma, 2012.

11 "*Allographic*" and "*autographic*" arts. In the context of an *allographic* work, what determines the validity of an object is its conformity to certain constitutive properties: variations do not engender – as long as these properties are respected – the invalidity or falsification of the object in question. In this sense, the reproduction of a poem in a color different from that of the original does not, for all that, engender the false character of the poem. A poem by Hölderlin written in red is just as authentic as the same poem written in black ink. On the contrary, autographic approaches integrate as part of their identity the history of the object and the modalities of its production. In an autographic approach the identity of the sample will be apprehended from the appreciation of its value and in the *allographic* approach its identity will be apprehended from the respect of a preliminary syntax: a preliminary notation or score. On this question: A. ANNE-BRAUN, *Le monde en projet: Une lecture de la théorie des symboles de Nelson Goodman*, PUPS, Paris, 2018.

situations. In this sense, "non-conceptual" would be everything that "goes without saying" and which, in this way, does not pose a problem to the mind.

When backed by custom, the fault would, for example, be "non-conceptual." The concept of fault would really appear when the new situation that should be characterised as faulty would be *scandalous* (and this when it would cause the old experience to stumble and would imply a questioning of a traditional non-reflexive consent).[12] It is, finally, a passage between the regularity (which is lived) and the rule that is followed (in accordance with a recognition that retroactively establishes a reason as a cause).

This precision is essential. Indeed, the meaning is delicate to apprehend, because it is torn between the denotation which is objective and the representations (which I have of the object of the meaning) which are subjective.[13] Moreover, in the field of law, there also appears a *deference* that offers experts the burden of meaning (the weight of the reference is transferred to the Other).

This question of meaning thus seems to express, for some, more a "property of consciousness"[14] (in the form of "the intention to signify") than a "property of language."[15]

According to us, the "meaning of the fault" could not be perfectly reconducted to the sum of its linguistic uses and to a simple linguistic grammar, because it appears continuously overwhelmed by the meaning given to it and manifests the presence of the meaning in the hollow of the meaning.[16]

12 Consent is thus understood as a freedom inscribed in the relationship to another. A freedom that would only be conditioned by the recognition of the other: the intellection of necessity, as it were, to use a Spinoza formula.

13 On this question the remarkable study: A. GALLERAND, *Husserl et le phénomène de la signification,* Vrin, Paris, 2014.

14 This question is related to the search for a kind of "mark of the mind." This search presents itself as a recurring problem in the philosophy of mind. Intentionality thus appears as one of its markers of the presence of the mind. Intentionality would, in this respect, make it possible to distinguish between mental phenomena and those that are not. Naturally, intentionality is not the only criterion that is likely to manifest this mark. Some authors thus consider that epistemological criteria such as "direct knowledge" or "first-person privilege" can also fulfil this function. Intentionality is, in this perspective, generally understood as "reference intentionality" (capacity of our thoughts to be "about") or "content intentionality" (propositional attitudes have a content, a meaning... therefore, they can represent states of affairs).

15 For analytic philosophy, the answer to this question is simple: when it comes to choosing between the "meaning of a statement" (for us implying the concept of fault) and facts that would be devoid of any meaning (for us the act of consciousness aimed at fault and its intentional correlate), the choice is obvious. All in all, there would thus be at the basis of the meaning of the fault and its uses, in the first case, a "linguistic grammar" and "language games" that would be proper to the implementation of this linguistic concept.

16 This thesis of the linguistic character of intentionality was defended, for example, by Ernst Tugendhat. For the philosopher of Czech origin, intentionality could, as it were, be reduced to a property of the verbs used and not to a particularity of thought itself. In this sense, Husserl would thus have only revealed, albeit in a new light, the transitivity of certain verbs. E. TUGENDHAT, *Conscience de soi et autodétermination*,

Meaning would only be the locus of this failure between subject of the statement and subject of the enunciation. What is given in the constitution of meaning is then the loss of the subject of the enunciation as body and presence in the utterance.

What we are going to try to extract, therefore, is no longer a "meaning of the fault" organised as a sum of uses, nor even the presence of an "essence" of the fault; but, more precisely, a "theme" and a "nature"[17] through which the "meaning" and significance of[18] the fault is given.

The fault should not, therefore, only be heard downstream of its linguistic translation through uses and "language games." It should be apprehended as an *objectivity* constituted with a certain aim and in accordance with a certain theme: the meaning of[19] fault would be given to the conscience "as such."

This nuance is important. Indeed, what will manifest itself immanent to consciousness will not be the material production of a physical object, but a categorical constitution: not an object, but in the language of Husserl[20] a reference, but from a construction that would be inherent to the reflexive structure of the intentional aim: the meaning of the fault is the fault aimed at "as such" from the agreement on various criteria. The fault is thus thematised in law and then naturalised on the basis of the act of language engaged in by a community of speakers agreeing on this theme.

The "legal fault" in its linguistic uses clearly implies the presence of two dimensions: the understanding of the *meaning of* the fault is inherent (it founds the theme); whereas the understanding of what the fault *manifests* would be empirical and external. It expresses the nature of the manifestation.

Armand Colin, Paris, 1995. More broadly on this debate: C. ROMANO, *Au cœur de la raison phénoménologique*, Gallimard, Paris, 2010. In particular, Chapter 3: "Les critères linguistiques de l'intentionnalité" pp. 104–133.

17 By the use of this term, we mean that the meaning of the fault must be situated, in order to be heard, in its natural space, that is to say, by this phenomenological approach in its very constitution, and this as meaning "as such."

18 He then distinguishes the latter from the "occurrences" that will be linked to this species or "type." The danger in this case was to make the species a material essence. The problem would be, however, the following: meaning cannot be an essence, because it is what finds its filling by objects. It is not an object, but that which makes it possible to relate to any object through such and such a sign. This is why, as early as 1908, the father of phenomenology abandoned the idea of signification as a "species" in favor of a more objective or noematic perception. In this Husserl resisted the pragmatic turn and refused to abandon the idea that it should be possible to relate signification to an object. However, this object is not a general object (such as a species or a type), but the object targeted "as such." This question is close, in law, to the one raised by Troper in his analyses of the meaning of the norm in Kelsen's thought. "If the norm is content, it has no content." M. TROPER, "Système juridique et État," in *Pour une théorie juridique de l'État*, PUF, Paris, 1994, p. 170.

19 GALLERAND, *Husserl et le phénomène de la signification*, Histoire de la philosophie, Vrin, Paris, 2014.

20 F. BRENTANO, *Psychologie du point de vue empirique*, Vrin, Paris, 2008. He was also influenced by Frege's influence, albeit more distant (G. FREGE, "Sens et dénotation," in *Écrits logiques et philosophiques*, Seuil, Paris, 1971) and Bolzano (concerning the work of Bolzano: the reference in France is the thesis of J. SEBESTIK, *Logique et mathématiques chez Bernard Bolzano*, Vrin, Paris, 1922).

The relationship to writing, a determining factor in the legal field, seems essential, because this documentary form will make it possible to fix meanings in signs and statements, and this over a certain period of time (in Bergson's sense): the articulation and coherence of legal discourse are thus *clues* in which meaning is given. Legal culture," "legal traditions," and "legal theories" are, for their part, the conceptual background that will allow the construction of a representation of the "objectivity" in question. The evolution of this concept of fault over time also demonstrates that this legal entity has a singularity within the framework of a certain social ontology: it is an incorporeal legal object (which, unlike objects that would be purely ideal, has a certain duration).[21] With regard to this duration, the object's appearance of diversity manifests an identity and a stability of a certain conceptual core allowing the species to be brought back to the genus.

A phenomenological analysis thus offers the interest of avoiding, on the one hand, the relativism peculiar to the psychological approach and, on the other hand, of responding to the impossibility (which seems inherent in psychological theory) of communicating meaning within the framework of an intersubjective relationship. This approach, finally, makes it possible to confront the classical question of an object's meaning that denotes nothing (the "ideal objects" different from the "real objects").

This meaning of fault will therefore, as a singular "categorical objectivity," be apprehended through the concepts that are likely to give it "as such" to our consciousness as a theme. It is therefore the relationship between the concept and the object that will now be important to us in order to bring out the intuition that allows the appearance of a knowledge of the meaning.

2 The "theme" inherent in the fault.

It will be necessary in order to allow the meaning of the fault to reach the rank of knowledge to "fill" it. In the sixth of the *Logical Investigations,* Husserl tries to accomplish this mission by means of "categorical intuition."[22] In this perspective, he will develop his famous analysis by spinning a metaphor between the full and the empty.

It is only when the act of service is "filled" [*Erfüllung*] by intuition that knowledge is formed.[23] The concept of filling (which, in this form, seems

21 *Cf.* G. LORINI, "Objets juridiques incorporels," in *Adolf Reinach entre droit et phénoménologie, op. cit.* p. 76. He quotes Reinach: "Recently we have begun to admit again, alongside the physical and the psychic, a specific type of ideal objects. But the essential character of these objects, such as numbers, concepts, propositions, etc., is their extra temporality.... Claims and obligations, on the contrary, last a certain interval of time, then disappear again. Thus, they seem to constitute objects of a new type, hitherto ignored."

22 *Logical Research.* In particular for "categorical intuition" in the 6th edition of the *Recherches Logiques.*

23 It appears, however, that in Husserl's thought this question of filling answers only the question of phenomenological evidence: how can one prove the evidence of something? His answer lies in this theory of knowledge and truth through the relevant filling by an intuition.

borrowed from Tarski) allows, moreover, to apprehend the *truth of* the aim of signification. This analysis is relatively easy to accept with regard to objects, targeted by the act of thinking, which have an empirical correlate. Nevertheless, it poses problems for Husserl as soon as the object that is aimed at remains without denotation,[24] as can be the case, in our hypothesis, with a judgment. This phenomenological orientation can be found in legal thought with the conception that makes the legal tool and the norm, a standard of capacity that makes it possible to measure a relationship (rendering an account of what it is possible to do). The latter accounts for a relationship not of strict identity but of equipment.

In fact, Husserl's path will guide him from a *noetic* concept (the object aimed at) of signification to a *noematic* concept of the latter (the aim itself): in the end, it will be a question of giving an account of the unity of signification elaborated from the diversity of real acts of consciousness. It will therefore be necessary to constitute this meaning (2.1) and then to examine its categorical form (2.2). All in all, it is thus in its thematic form that fault is formed.

2.1 The constitution of "the meaning of the fault"

In the first place, it is about supprimer apprehending the meaning as fulfilment. How does this fulfillment manifest itself in the framework of ideal objects and in our case of the faulty object? What Husserl will thus bring out to compensate for the absence of this sensitive intuition is that the meaning of these ideal objects[25] could be explained in accordance with a kind of *a priori* "logical grammar." It would be through the latter that we would relate to the thing. The Austrian philosopher sees, in this way, the presence of laws of thought that relate to what he calls the "categorical" which allows these laws to be *constituted* and therefore covers the field of what can be thought. In this sense, it is a question of founding the concept in a structure that would be inherent in it. This structure would be constitutive through retroactive performativity. It is the inscription in this concept that retroactively founds and constitutes the meaning. The meaning would be only the singular manner in which one relates to the thing "as" and through the acts wich express it.

24 Furthermore, Husserl rejects the idea of thinking of these ideal objects as fictions; that is, ultimately, as objects that are autonomous with respect to sensibility and without being filled by intuition, and that "pretend" that this relationship exists.

25 A relation between two objects in the world or in a "categorical" form (a name or a concept); the signification, which is a "categorical objectivity" (the object as it is thought: that is, the correlate of an activity and not the object that is thought or the psychic and linguistic experiences by which it is lived or expressed). The "meaning of the fault" thus refers not to a situation but to a situation apprehended as faulty. It is not a feeling but an ideal intentional unity. There is with fault a specific way of thinking about a state of affairs. We will see that the analysis of the apology, for example, is likely to reveal this identity. The apology, as the implementation of a strategy of justification, makes it possible to place in the light the machinery of action and judgments.

More specifically, it will be a question of becoming aware of the fault's meaning as constructed on the basis of a *logical* rationalization relating to a[26] synthetic[27] or *a priori* "state of things."

This analysis overlaps to some extent with the distinction Professor A. Tale made between *eidological* and *eidonomical*.[28] An *eidological* approach to the juridical act implies that the meaning of the act is independent of the norm and that the production of its effects is immediate. An *eidonomical* approach considers, for its part, that it is the *nomos* and not the *logos* that determine the meaning (the legal act's effects are then mediatised by the presence of a norm or a set of norms).[29] *Logos* [the reason] as well as *nomos* [the rule] would be likely to generate the partial intentions allowing, by overlapping, the birth of a categorical intuition. Two potential declinations of the categorical objectivity that forms the meaning of the fault thus appear. We can see that this objectivity has an ontological significance: it is constitutive (it is even retroactively constitutive).

The first approach is also evident in the work of Reinach.[30] It is a question of apprehending meaning through – or in – social ontology itself. The *a priori* grammar of fault would be the manifestation of the logical impossibility of associating together the object and the subject: the fault would supprimer in a certain way be inherent in a certain appearance of the world for the benefit of a subject who would make the world an object different from him. The diversity of faults would be the expression of the difficulty of "closing" the concept inherent in this debt imposed on us by the fact of existing in a social reality (the analytic of this concept would be infinite).[31] The fault

26 *Distinction* should be *made* between "states of things" [*Sachverhalt*] and "situation of things" [*Sachlage*]. The understanding is quite simple: for example, when "I look at a house" there is a primary intention ("I look at a wall of the house"), but this primary intention is articulated with partial intentions that do not necessarily have a sensitive intuition capable of fulfilling them (I do not see the walls opposite the one I am looking at, for example). But the totality of the intentions overlap in a flow.

27 Husserl will also demonstrate that this "categorical" intuition is "founded" on other acts (and in particular, primitively on the sensitive intuition). It is on the basis of certain given real objects (and by the play of various syntheses) that the ideal object will be constituted: it will thus not be given but founded. In this sense, it manifests: either relations, relations between objects (this is the syntactic approach); or content, but without an empirical instantiation (and this on a categorical basis: this is the case of a name, for example). Categorical objects are, in this perspective, of two types: they are syntheses or concepts. In this way, the fault is presented as a categorical object of a higher degree of intuition (more complex than real objects linked to a sensitive intuition).

28 CONTE, "Phenomena of phenomena," in *Interpretation and Epistemology. Acts of the VII Colloquium on Interpretation*, Galli, Turin, 1986, pp. 167–198. On the same question: L. PASSERINI GLAZEL, "Eidologico ed eidonomico nella fenomenologia dell'atto giuridico," in *Atto norma tipo tra pragmatica e ontologia del diritto*, Aracne, Rome, 2012, pp. 87–110.

29 PASSINI GLAZEL, *op. cit.*

30 REINACH, *Les fondements* a priori *du droit civil*, Vrin, Paris, 2004.

31 In the way in which for Hegel the identity A=A, that is to say the tautology, always masks with the paradox of identity the idea that identity is finally only the inscription of a lack in a name.

would be constituted on this initial and *a priori* intuition of a remnant that would always manifest a debt. This would be the explanation of the linguistic connection between fault, debt, and duty that we have previously pointed out and that seems to be found in all languages.

This *eidological* approach has been criticised by Czelaw Znamierowski who will thus oppose Reinach by advocating, for his part, an *eidonomic* approach.[32]

For the Polish philosopher, the concept would rest on the necessary presence of a set of thetical norms. According to the *eidonomic* approach, it is through the norm that certain activities receive meaning. It is as constructed by a norm that the state of things finds its meaning and can be properly fulfilled. Categorical intuition could thus be elaborated through these two formulas. Some believe that the purely *eidological* approach favors the analysis of experiences linked to objects (states of things). An approach according to which meaning would be inherent in the way in which we normalise our behavior in our relationship to objects would perhaps be more likely to integrate into this categorical intuition other modalities of experience such as affective tonalities that are important in the analysis of fault. "There is a timeless and universal common affective fund (love, hatred, anguish, joy, sadness, hope, suffering) ... inherent in the human condition"[33] which should also make it possible to thematise fault.

2.2 The categorical form of the "meaning of the fault": the manifestation of a theme[34]

The intentional object will thus be apprehended "as such" and this through the concepts that allow us to grasp it in some of its aspects. It will thus be freed from its ontological weight. As J. Benoit observes, "there is thus a categorical aspect wherever there is the possibility of a complete variable from the point of view of the form concerned."[35] The categorical manifests itself with the possibility thus offered "to conform an object independently of its content."[36]

32 L. PASSERINI GLAZEL, "Eidologico ed eidonomico nella phenomenologia dell 'atto guiridico'," in *Atto, norma tipo: Tra pragmatica e ontologia del diritto*, Aracne, Rome, 2012.

33 Cf. A. GALLERAND, *op. cit.* p. 213.

34 The object is constituted intentionally *as* the theme of the activity of consciousness. To return to the example that concerns us, that of the fault, we could say that this name is the object of a constitution; that it elaborates an objectivity that fixes the theme that accounts for the activity of the consciousness when we refer to it for a meaning. However, the persistence of this objectivity in time and in the reiterations to which it will be subjected testifies to its transcendence. It is the intentional unity of a multiplicity of acts: "the objectivity aimed at receives the meaning of a transcendent being in and through the repetition of the categorical activity itself." A. GALLERAND, *Husserl et le phénomène de la signification*, Vrin, Paris 2014, p. 184.

35 J. BENOIST, *Phénoménologie, sémantique, ontologie: Husserl et la tradition logique autrichienne*, Épiméthée, PUF, Paris, 2015, p. 112.

36 *Idem*

It is not simply a matter of representing a state of affairs in consciousness, but of aiming at it and constituting it through the "theme." The state of things that may be the logical basis of the fault is therefore not an "object of the world," but a construction on it through the theme.

It should be noted, as Professor Renaudie observes, that: "for the real to be given to us in such a way that it comes to make true the proposition that aims at it, it must be given to us in the very forms of meaning."[37] The theory of intuitive filling thus imposes to apprehend the denotation in relation to the very forms of the aim.

It is thus through the very *substance of* the concept[38] of itself. The latter appears as truly forming an act of production of consciousness. Consciousness will, in a predicative process, bring together and connect elements to form a "state of things" in accordance with a complete setting in variable of the form concerned. As soon as this state of things is constructed, I will be able to come back to the way in which things have been determined "as." It is thus necessary to re-enter what is judged as such. The faulty relation will acquire a meaning, a sense, in the capacity of the consciousness to retroactively grasp this object as a fault.

It is easy to see on examination that consciousness is phenomenal. In this sense, it masks "nothing." In fact, it presents itself not as a substance, but as a modality of appearance.[39] In the same way, it is the way in which a system codes itself (its *autopoietic* function) that pushes the latter to apprehend certain determinations as admissible motivations (what is invisible to the system, because of the way it functions and the way it codes itself and manufactures itself, is its "true" social function with regard to the whole that social reality forms). This is what Lacan expresses, in his own way, when he develops the idea according to which: in each affirmation is inscribed the position of enunciation of the subject. The "declaration" is always the "as such" capable of determining a truly human position (as a specific 'being'). This reflexivity allows, for example, the integration of temporality. The meaning of the fault "as" can, therefore, keep its unity over time.

This approach is likely to provide us with the means to think about the faulty hypotheses that could be virtually realised: "gross misconduct," "simple

37 J.M. RENAUDIE, "L'être et le sens des états de choses: Recherches Logiques," in J. BENOIST, ed., *Propositions et états de choses: entre être et sens*, Vrin, Paris, 2006, pp. 130–131.

38 In the language of Husserl this concept will work by abstraction. There is thus a sensible abstraction and a categorical abstraction. The sensitive abstraction manifests itself when, for example, one tries to isolate a part of a whole (for certain concepts of colors: "the green of this house" or "the red of this apple"). The general abstraction would reside in the idea of a green or a red in general. It is understood that what is abstracted in this case is the sensible itself.

39 From then on, the unconscious would be, for example, only a simple illustration of what Kant analysed as being of the order of "infinite judgment" – it would be inherent to the psyche and to the very development of this reflexive consciousness (it should be remembered that a judgment in which the predicate has a negative prefix must be distinguished from a judgment in which the predicate is itself negative: it is the difference between "X is undead" and "X is immortal").

misconduct," "serious misconduct," "inexcusable misconduct," "service misconduct" just as their variations and evolutions were the subject of a confrontation with the identity of categorical objectivity.

It is, in fact, in the *repetition of* this categorical objectivity.[40,41] The fault lies in "all times" and not in an essence that is "outside time." The meaning of the fault expresses an identity that manifests itself in time.

Once the concepts of fault and meaning clarified, it remains necessary to examine how the categorical that is at issue in this meaning is expressed and what its nature is.

3 Agreement on the "nature" of the fault

This last part will examine how to move from the meaning *of* the fault to the examination of its *meaning.*

This meaning is formed by the specific way in which a concept is always hailed in its relation to the world by a nature (by this we mean a specific way of agreeing on criteria in a form of life). It is this relationship (the connotation) that forms the meaning. There is thus an immanence of meaning in life and in the temporality of the world. It is in accordance with this approach that we can speak of a "nature" of fault. It should be noted that this relationship is both the condition for the construction of meaning and its limit: the problem and the answer.

This question is also expressed in the analysis of concepts. The latter is never totally in a relation of representation of the world, but what allows us to think a *relation to* the world.

When we know that we are doing something meaningful, we implement a concept with relevance.[42] In the end, the concept is only practical knowledge. The concept is its own reason: the "reason" for the rule it sets up.[43] As such, it seems to be the obvious basis of our relationship.

It is thus necessary to distinguish in the concept two aspects that are sometimes difficult to separate. The concept seems, at times, to be mechanically applicable and offers a measure of identity in relation to the world. A second aspect seems more enigmatic. There is, in fact, in the concept a part of true

40 Ultimately, this term is used to describe the state of affairs as such. Fundamental forms for objectivity.

41 GALLERAND, *Husserl…, op. cit,* p. 203.

42 *Tractatus* does not tell us much about what thinking itself can be. This is the previously mentioned problem of the "marker of the mind." Some analyses do appear, however, such as the one found at the heart of proposition 4 according to which: "Thought is a proposition endowed with meaning" or the earlier one according to which "the propositional sign used, thought, is thought." In this perspective, what is apparent is the link present for the Austrian philosopher between proposition and its form and thought. In this sense, thought is a kind of logical image of facts.

43 On this question: for a synthetic analysis J. BOUVERESSE, "Les raisons et les causes" *in Philosophie, mythologie et pseudo science, Wittgenstein lecteur de Freud*, 2nd ed., Éditions de l'Éclat, Paris, 2015.

(and inevitable) thought and not only a mechanical application.[44] The concept is never indifferent to the thought that applies it. In this sense, the concept is that particular place where we can think about the relationship between the identity of a thing (for example: the identity of the meaning of the fault) and the difference (the play of its variations over time). The concept is then presented as a norm or a standard of capacity. It is a question of measuring the way in which reality is molded within the mental tool. We find ourselves in front of a mechanism of apparatus. This is a standard in the sense in which Professor Amselek understands this notion: a tool to guide human action.

In this sense, the concept is that place where it is possible to agree on the normativity of the concept based on a reflection on these criteria. As Benedict observes following Bouveresse, this does not consist in stating that the concept is arbitrary, but only to indicate that it is its own reason.[45]

In this sense, the meaning of fault, in a phenomenological perception, implies, as we have seen, the constitution of a categorical objectivity that offers the possibility of aiming at fault "as such" by agreeing on certain criteria inherent in a form of life. This inclusion of the aim in the form of life will be the nature through which the unity of this meaning will be constituted.

This shaping of the horizon of variations in the meaning of the fault will appear as a conceptual form. If the concept only appears where I *consciously* know what I am doing, it implies a return to its normativity (on the apparatus or on the device). In a way, this will be negotiated over time – from this additional characteristic that I will have to negotiate – in order to maintain the identity of the categorical objectivity.

Negotiating the meaning of fault in one's identity (it is of all times and not out of time) implies in itself an agreement on its criteria.

Altogether, these seem to be the true level of analysis of our commitment to the concept. Their functioning is thus as transparent as it is essential. It is not in concepts that normativity lies. The deepest part of its examination would paradoxically be what seems to be a surface effect: agreement in judgments through the interplay of criteria.

44 In his book *Concepts* J. Benoist's conclusion offers a particularly enlightening example of this situation. "The city of Chicago has installed cameras at red lights. When a car passes by, it triggers the camera. At first glance, the situation is simple: the vehicle passes or does not pass; if it passes, it causes a photograph and, on this basis, the fine can be sent.... But this, as we know, is not enough. This principle of sharing, whose technical device seems, so to speak, to be the executor, as such, is abstract and therefore out of step with the reality to which it must be applied. A margin had therefore to be preserved by human intervention in the process. In a *violation* control center *reviewers* examine the clichés.... Drivers regularly trigger the cameras without any violations – often by stopping just after the stop line, or stopping abruptly after an acceleration – it is then up to the violation reviewers to determine whether they think there has been a violation." J. BENOIST, *Concepts: Introduction to Analysis*, Cerf, Paris, 2010, p. 174.

45 J. BENOIST, *Concepts, op. cit.*, p. 177.

This analysis of the meaning of the fault naturally poses the problem of logical or conceptual *a priori*. Far from settling the debate between the acceptance of a material *a priori* (a kind of "logical grammar") and a purely linguistic *a priori* (a grammar in our way of speaking rather than thinking), it is possible to find a middle ground.

With the idea of a "form of life" as expressed by S. Cavell's rereading of Wittgenstein, it is possible to hear both the idea of "form" and "life." The complex relations between reality, thought and language would then have two inseparable and complementary dimensions: a conventional form that would find its meaning in the very movements of life itself: the game proper to the actualization of its differences.

It would then be possible to consider two openings with regard to the meaning of the fault.

On the one hand, an attempt at logical or linguistic modeling from a deontic or semiotic algebra according to the models traced by J.L. Gardiès[46] or A.G. Conte.[47]

On the other hand, an analysis from a kind of ordinary language. It would be a question of rediscovering what J.-L. Austin[48] presented as a "linguistic phenomenology."

We will only open up a few avenues in this second orientation. The famous text by J.-L. Austin – which deals with apologies[49] – offers some possibilities in this regard. This text seeks to place in full light the ordinariness of our actions and the machinery of our actions. This question is essential in the field of fault and its meaning because it offers the possibility of understanding, from the inside, how faults are experienced and what they mean when we relate to them. There is, for example, a considerable difference between justification and the implementation of a true apology. With justification it is a matter of recognizing that the action that was taken was an action that had to be taken: there is therefore no fault, but reasons for taking an action. There is nothing that is missed in the action taken. With justification we accept responsibility while denying that what was done was wrong. With excuses the logic is different: we recognise in this hypothesis the bad character of our action, but we reject partially or totally the responsibility. The apologies show in fact, that man is always in the presence of the body, an invading body that I take everywhere and that he can be independently of my mind the efficient cause of my actions.

In this case, the nature of the fault seems to be brought to light. The fault expresses and manifests the theme – or the nature – proper to the inscription of an identity or an act in a symbolic order offered to the duration. This is the manifestation of what Hegel presents as a speculative identity: the identity of a form inherent in the dialectical totality of the necessarily reciprocal moments that constitute it. In this impossible identity, fault expresses the failure or the failure of a

46 GARDIES, *Essai sur les fondements, op. cit.*

47 *Cf.* the three-volume *Philosophy of normative language*, Giappichelli,Turin.

48 J.-L. AUSTIN, "Plaidoyer pour les excuses," in *Écrits philosophiques*, Seuil, Paris, 1994, p. 145.

49 J.-L. AUSTIN, "Plaidoyer pour les excuses," *op cit.*, pp. 136–170.

perfect reflexivity of identity. In the same way that the expression "the law is the law" manifests the presence of an authority that is ultimately external to this identity and which is only the manifestation of force itself. The expression "the fault is a simple or serious fault" expresses a contrario the idea that the identity of the fault itself is only what I add to the fault in order to qualify it: the fault "as such" is always that gap proper to the identity of a thing in relation to itself when it is projected into the duration of social life.

What the ordinariness of our language strategies demonstrates with respect to the meaning of fault is that fault must be understood as playing within a logical structure that opposes "good" and "bad" and the acceptance or not of responsibility (that the individual perceives without always fully understanding its dimension). It is then a question of two different logical structures which manifest themselves in the ordinary language, one dealing with individual values and the second with a relationship to the other – according to which the individual must answer for his or her behavior. The meaning of the fault will thus be, at each new occurrence, negotiated and rethought from its categorical horizon. In this way, the meaning of the fault always carries an implicit halo of the unthought. It is this way in which the individual more or less succeeds in relating to the idea he has of the Other's injunction that would constitute the nature of the fault.

This meaning does not reveal an *essence*, but a *nature* which is actualised. This nature "is the set of threads[50] by which the concept is already attached to reality."[51] It is this reality and the logic inherent in its construction which then appears as the natural ground from which the identity of the concept and the variation of its interpretations play out. It is this "nature" which then manifests itself as the truth[52] proper to the meaning of the fault.

50 *Cf.* TALE as to the presentation of fault as reflecting a conceptual "family likeness."
51 J. BENOIST, *Concepts, op. cit.*, p. 185.
52 *Cf.* A.G. CONTE, "Three senses of truth: semantic sense, eidetic sense, epistemic sense," in *Philosophy of normative language*, Giappichelli, Turin, 2001, pp. 1003–1008.

5 "Dispositional concepts" in law

Our challenge in this text will be to account for the influence of "dispositional concepts" in legal discourse. Indeed, this categorization seems to us likely to do justice to certain mysteries that seem inherent in normativity. In order to account for this discovery, we will first attempt to clarify what should be understood the terms "dispositional concepts" in law (I); secondly we will seek, to identify the consequences inherent in this effort to create a conceptual framework based on the use of some of these terms in the explanation of what normativity is (II).

I An epistemic clarification of dispositional concepts in law

In this first part, we will try to identify the conditions relating to the appearance of a new conceptual category. This effort implies clarifying the meaning we give to certain terms. It will be a question, in particular, of specifying this meaning in the legal field, and this as soon as this category appears only under a variation of the conceptual genre. Later, we will specify the singularity of dispositional concepts. In our view, this lies in the fact that they crystallise a certain dispositional equilibrium (or make visible a dispositional "field"). Thus, we could say that concepts are normative by their relevance (A) and that normativity is itself the relevance of the dispositional concept (B).

A The "concepts," the "legal concepts" and their relevance

It seems necessary, in a preliminary way, to specify the relationship (or orientation) of the concept with respect to the world. Traditionally, concepts are oriented towards the world[1] in two senses: either they are the prerequisite of the world; or, they are deduced from the world. we understand that these two orientations are linked. They express two moments that are reciprocally necessary in relation to our relationship to the world: perception and explanation. In fact, a concept does not necessarily develop *a priori* (as the famous "conceptual glasses" theory might

1 To agree on this term: cf. J. RABACHOU, *Qu'est-ce qu'un monde?* Vrin, Paris, 2016. This question is ontological and applies to the totality of what exists. This naturally raises the question inherent in the definition of what exists.

DOI: 10.4324/9781003130109-6

suggest). It also derives and develops from the world it is supposed to account for. It does not thus express a reality which is prior to thought and language and which would be "already there" but must have a relationship of relevance and adequacy with the reality for which it is intended.[2]

Therefore, it is imperative to distinguish, on the one hand, the fact that conceptual thinking takes place *in the* always contextual reality of a given situation and that, on the other hand, it is not the way to access this situation. It is, in this sense, only the manifestation of our capacity to apprehend a situation "in a given form."[3] Conceptual thinking is not the mirror of the world but a shaping of the world (a presentation of it) from a given angle. There is, very clearly, the challenge of a certain magical thinking that would relate to reality.

In addition, we know that we don't need to conceptualise "everything." It is obvious that the need to discriminate (through the use of the concept) really appears only when our relationship to the world becomes, in part, "absurd."

This explains, in our opinion, the unfortunately tautological definition of "functional concepts." Indeed, all concepts have a discriminating function and seek to answer a question. Thus, there is a clear link between our need for meaning and direction in our relationship to the world [which, because of the presence of language, has become more difficult because it is less direct] and the presence of a concept or its emergence. In fact, the individual understood as a "speaking being" (and as such eminently social) is lost in language, that is to say in a normally oriented representation of the world. The loss of meaning is clearly inherent in this capacity to question one's relationship to the world.

The concept is therefore not bound by *reference to* the world. It is not intended to denote something of the world.[4] It would only be a way of refusing the presence of the world in language in favor of something that is "already there": a mythological world language would refer to. An ordering of the world would thus be preferred to the analysis of the thought that constitutes it. This thought is itself woven into the world. In fact, language appears as the gift of the

2 It is the bet of a certain pragmatism which presents itself as a practical philosophy and an anti-essentialism or representationalism: a philosophy of action. See J.-P. COMETTI, *Qu'est-ce que le pragmatisme*, Gallimard, Paris, 2010. Relevance is not to be found in the representation of the object of the concept: the intelligence of the concept is in the action and in its pragmatic acceptance. Moreover, it is not possible to get out of language all the data are thus linked to a "version of the world" (Goodman): to a "language game" (Wittgenstein) of a certain contextualism which thus offers the capacity to go beyond the purely semantic approach of a meaning to the benefit of a pragmatic approach that allows one to free oneself from a certain representationalism (in these various forms: strong or weak or minimalist literality: *cf.* F. RECANATI, *La transparence et l'énonciation*, Seuil, Paris, 1979 and the rest of his work).

3 As Professor BENOIST perfectly observes in his book *L'adresse du réel*, Vrin, Paris, p. 21: one cannot think a thing without thinking it in a certain way.

4 The question of the concept is not that of our relationship to the world or the contact that can be established with reality through the concept. By nature we are always in the world and the mystery is paradoxically that we may have the strange sensation or the strange weakness of forgetting it for a moment.

world itself. It is man's "form of life" from which he cannot hope to escape. It is thus when individuals find themselves disoriented *in* this form of life that concepts appear. These are not a specific access to the world, but seem to be constitutive of it. They are, as such, affected by the evolution of the "life form" and by a certain conceptual holism subject to various transformations and evolutions.[5]

In this sense, the concept does not seem to be, solely, of the order of the symbolic and representation. It is therefore not of the order of semantics. Its mystery seems, obviously, to lie beyond this analysis. There is more than a simple convention in the concept. What seems to manifest itself is a link of relevance that is woven into the reality of a situation and this through an experience.

It is, with the concept, a specific way to catch the real. This capacity seems to develop fully from it. To say it in a different way, the concept applies itself to think the world from the world itself (and this in the way, always singular, which is proper to those who will have to enunciate it).[6]

It is clearly on this basis that the question of its relevance must be asked.

A concept is relevant when it offers us the possibility of answering a question or when it offers the capacity of our mind to give "meaning" to the world and to walk within it. Not just a simple meaning, but more broadly meaning. In this way, it encourages action and the emergence of the rule. Its appearance – or its use – seems to answer this question of relevance.

It is in this specific register that the presence of legal concepts is manifested.

These appear to be inherent in a language of specialty: positive law. Legal language has the vocation to express two singular aspects: it calls for *deference* and it appears as a discourse of implementation.

It is, in the first place, a language in which meaning manifests itself by *deference*. The meaning of legal terms is thus referred to experts. A community of experts engages, through it, in a certain relationship to the world and to language and agrees *on* and *in* its use. If one accepts the idea that the concept does not *represent* anything specific, then the question arises as to what it *expresses*.[7] The legal

5 Quine analysed this situation perfectly. For him, for example, science is an extension of common sense; it is not inherently different from it and as such it uses the same strategy: inflating ontology to simplify theory. From then on, at the periphery of the experiment, adjustments are possible with respect to the theoretical field, but care must be taken to deform the overall theoretical system as little as possible in order to respect a principle of economy.

6 The philosophy of language must be articulated from a triangle whose vertices are: the world, the mind, and language. In this sense, language expresses something of the world. As such, various theses are possible: language can express something of the world through a denotation but also a convention, a psychological fact or a kind of code of thought, the ordinary of the world itself, a set of language practices (language would in this sense be a kind of specific modeling of these practices) etc.

7 The theory of law could make good use of these analyses: positivism apprehends law as a body of rules, criticism of this analysis (the most classical) manifests itself with the realists who bring up the question of interpretation, the hermeneutic current will then bring its stone to the edifice by criticizing the composition of law from the "rules" by introducing the "principles" into the game of law. Finally, pragmatics tends to modify this approach, which tended to be purely semantic, for the benefit of a true pragmatics

concept expresses a specific agreement on what is, ideologically, law. The law would then be relation inherent in a practice. This *deference* seems, naturally, to be related to the relevance of the concepts.[8] A concept is therefore related to a certain functional understanding of our relationship to the world. Therefore, the emergence of a new concept is always linked to a certain collapse of older concepts that appear to engage in a certain crisis (such as the concept of the State or the concept of community).[9] The concept is, in this respect, only "practical knowledge." It reveals, from a reality, a norm that offers to think about reality from a certain angle. The concept is in itself *its* reason. It is "the reason" for the rule it installs and invents.[10] It thus states a "thing" that is more or less clearly understood by the community of those who use it.

Second, the legal discourse, as it manifests itself in the specialised language of jurists, expresses a work of accompaniment of power. Bourdieu understood this situation perfectly. The work of rationalization of legal operators offers the possibility of the coexistence of various registers of enunciations that are mutually supportive and thus form a system:

> Jurists are very interested in this work [of rationalization], they are stakeholders since, in the elementary forms of division of labour of domination, one of the first agents outside the royal family is the jurist: jurists are very interested both in legitimizing and legitimizing themselves and in empowering themselves through the power of legitimization they have to legitimize royalty in order to legitimize themselves as capable, for example, of reprimanding the king.... But part of the legal work is to accompany the exercise of power.[11]

Finally, it is a matter of making various registers of enunciation coexist and converge. This question of the articulation of enunciations has been perfectly explained by the French anthropologist:[12]

that should lead us to modify our conception of the "rule of recognition" and the social actors that are included in it.

8 This question of thinking is a delicate one. We know, for example, that the *Tractatus* does not tell us much about what thinking is in itself. Some analyses, such as the one found at the heart of Proposition 4 according to which: "Thought is a proposition endowed with meaning" or the earlier one according to which "the propositional sign used, thought, is thought," in this perspective what manifests itself is the link present for the Austrian philosopher between the proposition and its form and thought. In this sense, thought is a kind of logical image of facts.

9 See note 5.

10 On this question: for a synthetic analysis J. BOUVERESSE, "Les raisons et les causes" in *Philosophie, mythologie et pseudo science, Wittgenstein lecteur de Freud*, 2nd ed., l'Eclat, Paris, 2015.

11 P. BOURDIEU, *Sur l'Etat: cours au collège de France 1989–1992*, Seuil, Paris, 2012, p. 391.

12 *Cf.* B. LATOUR, "Petite philosophie de l'énonciation," *Dits et inédits*, 2002.

> The enunciation is an act of sending, of mediation, of delegation. This is what its etymology says *ex-nuncius*, to send a messenger, a nuncio ... we can now define enunciation: the set of acts of mediation whose presence is necessary in the sense; although absent from the enunciations the trace of their necessary presence remains marked or inscribed, so that it can be induced or deduced from the movement of the enunciations. There are marks of enunciation like magnetism that the lava rejected by volcanoes and the faults of the earth keeps as it cools. Although nothing from the outside betrays their magnetic past, it is possible, millions of years later, by interrogating the rocks with a magnetometer, to find the trace, faithfully kept, of the orientation of the magnetic pole, as it was on the day of the eruption.

The relevance of the concepts thus depends on their capacity to adequately standardise a certain relationship to the world and this for the benefit of a dominant discourse.

It is now necessary to distinguish the singularity of "dispositional concepts" and to analyze their relevance in the legal use of the concepts.

B Dispositional concepts and normativity as a concept

In this section, we will therefore attempt to determine what should be specifically understood by "dispositional concepts" (B1). Subsequently, we will seek to highlight how this category is able to make normativity explicit (B2).

B1

Within the terminology inherent in logical empiricism,[13] it is common to consider a "dispositional predicate" as the one that does not describe a character that immediately presents itself as observable. On the contrary, the dispositional predicate presents itself as a regularity. This manifested by events (or behaviors) under specifically appropriate conditions.

In this sense, the dispositional predicate expresses the singular way in which a thing is accustomed to react to a given context.

13 Logical empiricism shows a revival of empiricism in the 19th century within the Austro-Hungarian Empire. This revival of empiricalist thought was sparked mainly by Ernst Mach and Moritz Schlick. This modern form of empiricism is linked to the development of the epistemology of the natural sciences. In the form of logical positivism, one will thus find within the Vienna Circle authors such as Carnap, Neurath, Hahn, etc. These authors sought to free themselves from the influence of metaphysics for the benefit of experience. It was against this logical positivism that Quine later developed his famous critique of the two dogmas of empiricism. Quine's objective was to demonstrate that the empiricism deployed by Carnap was incompatible with the double pretension of rejecting this metaphysics and of separating tautologies and synthetic propositions.

Traditionally, the philosophy of science tended to banish them. This was logical since it was not possible to attribute a purely empirical meaning to them. In the scientific field, this obscuring of provisions was presented in the form of a desire to "reduce" provisions. The aim was to reduce this question (of powers or dispositions to use scientific terms) to a simple epistemological or semantic question. Indeed, if it is possible, as Bergson's analysis suggests, to see a sugar cube dissolve over *time,* it was considered impossible to observe "solubility" itself. It is according to the same logic that Molière made fun of "the sleeping virtue of opium."[14]

The "powers" and "virtues" appeared, it is easy to understand, as relics and after-effects of a magical and archaic thought that modern science had to make disappear.

This scientific ostracism seems today clearly challenged by various aspects of the development of science.

This rebirth of dispositions is particularly evident in the evolutions of contemporary physics and in the inherent analysis, for example, of "elementary particles." These, by definition, do not integrate other (more elementary) particles and do not present themselves as having a structure that could explain the disposition. They are not a simple effect of an underlying structure. A structure which, in the end, would be the substance or basis[15].

In accordance with, this development, it can be seen, at present, that provisions can be understood as properties of things related to their "possibilities of being." They would therefore be linked to the order of what is possible for the things in question.[16] Thus, these dispositions (even if they are not observable) would nevertheless be real. According to some, it is perhaps even the totality of reality that would be constituted in this form.[17] Quantum physics obviously tends in this direction and actualises Leibniz' famous intuition of a certain "pre-established harmony" between monads that would be so arranged towards each other. This very contemporary branch of physics thus uses dispositions and largely neglects substances.

Once the provisions are considered real, it must be admitted that the concept of disposition then implies a certain force. The obvious fact (as the logical result of the foregoing) is that the disposition is an entity endowed with truly causal power. What is done by the dispositional object in the world is thus realised from its singular disposition. Here, for example, there are obvious links with the theory of *affordance*[18] in the psychological field.

14 MOLIÈRE, *Le malade imaginaire.*

15 A parallel evolution can be found within the framework of the philosophy of mind with the highlighting of the failure of internalism and within the framework of probability theory and the rapprochement between the concepts of propensity and disposition.

16 It is a modality of being.

17 This is finally what field theory seems to evoke within the framework of quantum physics.

18 Theory developed in the field of psychology, for example, by J.J. Gibson. In order to understand this theory properly it is necessary to start from the meaning of the English term which must be translated as offering or being able to do something.

This approach is also found in contemporary philosophy in the framework of "dispositional realism."[19] This thesis naturally finds antecedents. It is possible, in fact, to find roots for this approach in the theories related to universals and in the classical opposition between Leibniz and Descartes.[20] We will, for our part, emphasise a determination that is perhaps less studied by philosophical doctrine and which seems to us more illustrative of this idea. The language of the ancient Greeks seems to have, naturally, integrated this situation. Unfortunately, the ordinary use of our contemporary language very often obscures this disposition of language as perceived by the ancients. There is thus a certain *disposition* specific to the human being – and which constitutes his form of life – which is manifested in the classical Greek language and which makes certain more contemporary languages disappear. The classical Greek language seems to be oriented towards a thought of the being based on the way it presents itself to the mind. For example, philosophy was like this

> This high knowledge [which] allows one to stand within the being, the storm of being as befits a man worthy of the name. *Philosophia*: the passion for the true knowledge that allows one to stand at the height of being, that which relates to *the alêtheia, to the* manifestation of being such as men have always

19 This dispositional realism is currently defended by Claudine Tiercelin, holder of the chair of Metaphysics and Philosophy of Knowledge at the Collège de France. In her book *le ciment des choses*, a small treatise on metaphysics, she will defend the idea of a metaphysics that is not really outdated. For her, this metaphysics has never ceased to exist in the sense that the history of philosophy or systems regularly raise this question. It therefore haunts a preponderant part of philosophy. There is only displacement of metaphysics. The idea is therefore to take up this question again for Tiercelin: metaphysics is only the examination of the properties of reality. This implies a reflection on the concepts and categories of our time. It is a question of going beyond reality as it gives itself in order to approach what is reality "in itself"; there is therefore a certain refutation of Kant's thought. This metaphysics will therefore be realistic and scientific. It would therefore be possible to develop a knowledge of metaphysics on the basis of a new model. Tiercelin's realism is opposed to fiction; it is a position of common sense that refutes relativism and idealism. Reality is at the same time something independent of what we think and at the same time it is relative to our thinking is real which means something real according to a semantic approach but the real is not reducible to that. For the French philosopher, there is a causal dynamic force of realism that manifests itself in the way the world is made. It is not a Platonic realism. The realism of dispositions implies that the physical universe contains dispositions as properties that are properties that are only perceived at the moment they manifest themselves. And yet they are always there. Contemporary physics seems to insist on these powers of things and less on categories. For Tiercelin, the danger of a transformation of this realism into metaphysics would reappear if our conception of the world were to focus only on these dispositions, erasing in a certain way the presence of the laws of nature. For her the dispositions are decisive and important but do not engender the disappearance of the laws that derive from the properties themselves. In this sense they are regularities rather than rules.

20 On this opposition, for example, M. GUEROULT, *Leibniz: dynamique et métaphysique*, Aubier, Paris, 1967.

> been called upon to face it. If the Greeks did not invent, certainly, the fact of being face to face with this opening or this deployment (this is the human adventure itself since the first day a human began to speak), they invented on the other hand the word that will designate the being of man and this being within which he has to find himself and find himself through speech and thought.[21]

The "being" would thus be a potential space that would be open to the manifestation of ***dispositions.*** Truth would then be an opening to the space of relations that founds it (it is this truth that language and the very grammar of language would seek to apprehend).

This question of the existence of a grammar[22] (and of the laws that would be inherent to it) poses, in a renewed way, a classic problem. It is the opposition between provisions and laws. Indeed, are relations internal (and contingent on the things that are put in relation and thus on their dispositions) or are they external and necessary and thus dependent on laws?

In an empirical approach, which has been now classical since Hume, natural law is understood as a regularity. Naturally, it is not, as such, considered causal. It does not give rise to internal links between events. It therefore seems to call into question the very idea of necessity (which is traditionally the basis and foundation of laws).

Various authors have, however, tried to save this relationship between regularity and law (and between contingency and necessity). For David Lewis, for example, it is possible to define natural law as a "generalization." He thus indicates that a natural law (which is "nomologically necessary") is actualised in all worlds that obey the same scientific laws. However, since it is contingent that "this world" is ours, what is nomologically necessary is then contingent. For him, "possible worlds" exist. More precisely, they coexist with our world. Our world, as such, is only actualised by our presence within it.

In this sense, the possibility is not a lack of actuality, but only an alternative to the actuality of another world. Therefore, there would be law only "if and only if" the latter can be axiomatically deduced from a systematization of facts that optimally combines strength and simplicity.[23]

This approach has been criticised (and amended) by various authors. This is the case, for example, in the famous "DTA" law.[24] According to this law, properties are universals and characteristics that are recognizable in space and time. The instantiation of a natural law would then be the relation between universals.

These different approaches (which have been quickly reviewed) allow to articulate the regularities and the ***a priori a priori*** antithetic idea of law.

21 B. SICHÈRE, *Aristote au soleil de l'être,* CNRS, Paris, 2018, p. 15.
22 In the sense of Wittgenstein.
23 D. LEWIS, *De la pluralité des mondes* (1986), L'éclat, Paris Tel-Aviv, 2007.
24 F. Dretske (1977), M. Tooley (1977) and D. Armstrong (1983).

It is now appropriate to ask whether this analysis (which takes place within the framework of natural law) is transposable within the framework of a social ontology and in the field of ethics?

We will try to show that moral or ethical *dispositions* can also be realistically analyzed without sinking into ethereal Platonism. The dispositions that the norms translate finally form a certain system of rationality that appears as a belief.

B2

The expression of a disposition as regularity (which is articulated in a field of relations) offers, in our opinion, to show the "form of life" inherent in man.

If the concepts are then normative, because they respond to this disposition proper to what man is (as entangled a subject in speech). Then normativity, itself, is elucidated by this disposition.

Normativity would account for human reality and would be actualised in the form of various regularities. This question of normativity would only reflect the dynamic and causal force of certain human and social dispositions.

This normativity would be intrinsic to a field and could, however, appear as a law. This would not be *a priori*, but could be deduced *a posteriori* from, for example, an axiomatization of regularities that would be discovered in the context of an investigation (in the pragmatic sense of the term).

Moreover, this pragmatic investigation will be, within the framework of the law, partly inherent to the use of language.

Legal concepts are thus "dispositional concepts." They highlight the reciprocal and updated action of various provisions. As such, they are normative.

Concepts set the rules. Implicitly and in the form of an agreement on criteria or explicitly in the form of a standard that determines whether the object is a relevant sample of the concept. They make it possible to apprehend "according to a certain meaning [the one offered precisely by the concept]" situations.

In this sense, thinking in its conceptual aspect offers to standardise the reality it institutes according to what its "disposition" is.

There is, then, an identity between "thinking a thing" and "applying to it the norms" inherent in the word we use in this way. From then on, a typicity (a category that mobilises certain concepts to give meaning to reality) seems to be logically normative.[25]

This question of normativity has become – even beyond law and legal theory – over the years one of the essential questions of contemporary philosophy. Within this framework, it is agreed that certain concepts seem to present themselves as

25 We know, according to a famous formula, that "thinking is classifying." *Cf.* J. BENOIST, *Concepts: introduction to analysis,* Cerf, Paris, 2010, in particular the chapter on the conceptual and the non-conceptual. But also on the difficulty of thinking and classifying differently: C. RAFFESTIN, "Penser et classer dans les sciences sociales," *Revue européenne des sciences sociales*, 42 (127) (2003). On this question in law: L. PASSERINI GLAZEL, *La forza normativa del typo, pramgatica dell'atto giuridico e teoria della catagorizzazione*, Quodlibet, Macerata, 2005.

normative. This class of normative concepts is understood as heterogeneous. Nevertheless, some groupings seem quite logical: evaluative or axiological[26] concepts, as well as deontic concepts, are clearly normative.[27] Beyond this classification, the question seems less obvious. From a pragmatic perspective, we consider that concepts are reality as they are normalised by them.

This disposition of concepts to explain normativity seems to be confirmed by the work of Davidson and Brandom. The two authors demonstrate, each in his own way, that it is not an external law that offers causality to men. There is an entanglement between all things that are related (and this by agreement of dispositions). There is a belief system that offers to believe in a certain "presumed rationality" in other people's behavior.

In this respect, it seems useful to refer to the "principle of charity" or "equivalence" as formalised by Davidson. This charity imposes the idea, quite classical in the field of psychoanalysis, according to which the subject is subject "for a signifier" and then finds meaning only in "the Other of the structure of language." Davidson adheres to a holistic conception of language. For him, language is the entire "Other." This holistic approach implies that meaning is indeterminate and that it can be traced back to all occurrences of the word within a discourse. It is therefore necessary to look at the functioning of the word in the order of discourse. In this logic, language does not *really* exist (it is only an ontological mirage). Only the *factory of* meaning exists. To understand is thus to interpret the other's statements. When I interpret, "I" is inclined to accept the idea of a systematic agreement of our beliefs and "I" accepts that in the place of the Other the meaning is thus deposited. The meaning of the concept is therefore the norm of my agreement with the Other and others. This analysis is perfectly compatible with the presence of a meaning "by deference" that would be inherent in a language of specialty.

In accordance with Davidson's work,[28] the "principle of charity" can be understood in the following form: he recommends interpreting a speaker's language on the assumption that the sentences he holds to be true are, as far as possible, true and that he is coherent and rational.

Davidson seeks to motivate this principle. He points out that the content of a belief is determined by its position in a belief system. This belief system makes it possible to identify what the belief is about. For example, a person cannot believe that a rabbit has just jumped down the rabbit hole without also believing that a rabbit is a small mammal with long ears and a small tail, of such and such a size, living in a burrow, and so on. It is not necessary that this

26 This implies, for example, the concept of "good governance" of the international financial institutions.

27 Ch. TAPPOLET, "La normativité des concepts évaluatifs," *Philosophiques*, 38 (2011), pp. 157–176.

28 This analysis is related to the work of Quine. Davidson thus developed an idea of semantic truth in 1967 in an article *Truth and meaning* using the concepts developed by Quine in *The word and the thing*. D. DAVIDSON, "On the Very Idea of a Conceptual Scheme," in *Inquiries into truth and interpretation*, Clarendon Press, Oxford, 1984, especially on the principle of charity pp. 267–289

person subscribe to a specific list of other beliefs in order to have the belief in question. Nevertheless, in order for a person's individual beliefs to be identified, it is necessary for that person to have a belief system in which we find primarily truths. Attributing too many false beliefs to a certain concept tends to make it impossible to identify the content of that concept.[29]

In the end with the implementation of this "principle of charity" it is a question of making explicit what will allow us to get along. It is a question of understanding ourselves, and this in the very experience of democracy (not understood as a political form but as a procedure). It is a question, finally, of thinking about our commitment in a new world and in a society that is no longer considered as the object of a reduction to unity.

In order to apprehend in a holistic context the thought of the other, it is thus necessary to consider it in a certain way as reasonable. This character will be apprehended with regard to a global system of beliefs. It is a matter of accepting the idea that society is one word and an infinity of things according to Dewey's formula. The belief in governance is thus postulated as true, coherent and rational. It is only at this price that "I" can come to terms with the old concepts. There is, in this way, in man's life form a disposition to agree wich is our reality and the true cement between things.

According to Davidson, semantic and intentional concepts are thus normative. In this sense, any concept will be associated with normative constraints that make it possible to establish which are the correct applications of the concept. In order to understand each other, the interlocutors must, for the most part, share the same set of beliefs. A divergence between beliefs ultimately masks only an adherence to a "background" belief. Talking about governance, for example, does not mean rejecting politics and its concepts, but on the contrary adhering to the renewed background of concepts inherent to politics. It is about experiencing politics and democracy no longer as a form of government, but as a form of life. This is a manifestation of a form of inter-passivity.[30]

These beliefs articulate various truths that are mutually reinforcing and rationally explained. They are based on the acceptance of the rationality of the other's thinking:

> According to Davidson, to be someone who believes, you have to be someone who interprets the discourse of others, but "*you can't fully explain either one's language or one's thinking, and neither has conceptual priority. The two are, of course, linked in the sense that each needs the other to be understood, but the link is not so complete that one of the two would be sufficient, even reasonably reinforced, to explain the other.*" DAVIDSON, 1993, p. 229.[31]

29 M. MONTMINY, "Normativité et irréductibilité du mental," *Dialectica*, 56 (4) (2002), p. 317.

30 According to this principle the action is reported on the structure wich acts in our place… the examples are numerous: the laughter recorded in television series, the prayer wheel or the candles in certain religions… These elements show how by the mere fact of postulating the existence of an Other, the latter can be charged with our action and thus guarantee us a certain passivity.

31 Cited by R. BRANDOM, *L'articulation des raisons: Introduction à l'inférentialisme,* Cerf, Paris, 2009, p. 15.

He will thus give "being" [to the situation as it is] its norm.

> The rules are standards of correction. They do not, for example, describe how people speak – they define what it means to speak correctly, i.e. in a meaningful way.[32]

This question, as we have said, is relatively classic. It is generally apprehended from the analysis offered by Wittgenstein in his *Philosophical Research*.[33]

It has given rise to what is generally presented as the "paradox of the rule."[34] This is expressed in the following way: following a rule is understood as conforming to one's *representation of* the rule. The Austrian philosopher links this question to the question of private language. This paradox is understandably focused on the fact that following the rule derives from an interpretation.

Beyond this first fact, two misunderstandings arise and reinforce the paradox. On the one hand, the rule is said to predate its application. On the other hand, the rule would be "internal." It would be present "in our head" or "in our mind" (a kind of soliloquy forming an idiolect generated by an isolated speaker and without the help of a dialect or the other members of the community). However, these misunderstandings can be corrected, and this, as long as one understands the rule as an apprenticeship and accepts the idea that the rule exists implicitly even before it is made explicit.

The question that arises, from this moment on, is to determine where the implicit normativity lies and how it manifests itself. The solution is that the rule exists in the world: it is what the actors agree on. In this sense, the rule exists: either in a certain "form of life";[35] or (as Brandom demonstrates in his work *Making it Explicit*[36]) in the "game of supply and demand of reasons."

32 H.-J. GLOCK, *Dictionnaire Wittgenstein*, Gallimard, Paris, 2003, entry "suivre une règle," p. 514 et seq.

33 L. WITTGENSTEIN, *Recherches philosophiques*, Gallimard, Paris, 2004.

34 This "follow a rule" question poses a challenge to the conceptual content of our statements. Saul Kripke interpreted Wittgenstein in this way by showing that no mental representation or behavioural disposition goes beyond itself. For each idea or behavioural disposition there are thus an infinite number of logically possible rules wich are all in agreement with that idea or disposition.

35 We know this question of the form of life dear to Wittgenstein and the more modern readings developed by S. Cavell. "We learn and teach words in certain contexts.... There is no guarantee that this projection will take place ... just as there is no guarantee that we will make and understand the same projections.... Just as there is no guarantee that we will make and understand the same projections. The fact that on the whole we do so is a matter of the shared path of our interests and feelings ... of what makes an enunciation and an assertion a call, an explanation – the whole organic whirlwind that Wittgenstein calls a 'form of life'. Language and human activity, health and human community are based on nothing more, and nothing less. This is a vision as simple as it is difficult, and as difficult as it is terrifying ... difficult because it is terrifying." S. CAVELL, "Le débat de l'ordinaire," in *Qu'est-ce que la philosophie Américaine*, Gallimard, Paris, 2009, p. 338.

36 For the French translation: R. BRANDOM, *Rendre explicite: Raisonnement, représentation et engagement discursif*, Cerf, Paris, 2010 (in two volumes).

In this approach the rule is, in the end, only the sum of these applications and its necessity is grammatical.[37]

The approach to the rule will therefore be inferential and should give rise to a study of the mechanisms and procedures within which it plays a normative role. This analysis of the rule is, of course, intimately intertwined with a realistic or pragmatic conception of the law. In this hypothesis, it will be a matter of rejecting law as the expression of a "backward world" or as the manifestation of a "must be" (in accordance, for example, with the various analyses linked to the presence of a "natural law"[38] or a "normativist positivism"). Law is not in the world of being or in minds. It is in minds that are in bodies, and the bodies themselves are in the world and are involved in relationships. What manifests itself in this passage is the appearance of a dialectic according to which a chain of inference is unraveled: here is the rather classical manifestation in Hegel's perspective of a kind of retroactive performativity. It is the discovery of this inferential chain that makes the antecedents appear as premises.

The normativity of this philosopher must be appreciated from a certain mutation due to the analysis of concepts. This philosopher of language will thus seek to question the concept of representation – which in a classical way was at the very heart of the analysis of language and this from the phenomenon of denotation.[39] For him, normativity is no longer anchored in a denotative relationship, but rather in the possibility of deriving the norm from an implicit social practice. This strategy developed by Brandom to circumvent the problems of representation and to base his normativity on the idea of a social norm is also constructed by avoiding two approaches that he deems unsuccessful: regulism (he analyzes himself in the fact of thinking that the explicit formulation of a rule can give rise to a norm[40]) and *regularism* (in this second approach, normativity would simply lead back to a

37 But the philosopher goes far beyond this logic, which would have nothing very original in view of the demonstration offered by a Wittgenstein II by Austin or by Searle. His originality lies in the association between pragmatics and semantics. It is the content of the proposal that interests Brandom.

38 On modern natural law: H.L.A. HART, *Law, liberty, and morality*, Stanford University Press, Stanford, 1963; D.N. MACCORMICK, "Natural law Reconsidered," *Oxford Journal of Legal Studies*, 1 (99) (1981) (on Finnis); WINSTON, K., ed., *The principles of social order. Selected essays of Lon L. Fuller*, Hart, London, 2002.

39 For Brandom the problem – it is the one he deals with mainly in the initial chapter (towards a normative pragmatics) of his magnum opus – lies in the impossibility from the outset to determine what the relation implementing the representation consists of.

40 "The properties of execution that are governed by explicit rules do not form an autonomous stratum of normative status, a stratum that could exist when no other stratum exists" p. 20. We know the criticism developed against this regulationism by means of the argument of regression to infinity. Wittgenstein thus considers that there is a way of grasping the rule that is not only interpretation. "The problem inherent in this type of regulationism was clearly identified by Kant but was formulated more incisively by Wittgenstein [...] an explicit rule cannot, by itself, determine the normative status of something else. It must be applied. But application is also something that can be done correctly or incorrectly. Therefore, there must be a second-order standard that specifies how first-order standards are to be applied. But then, how are these

regularity of behaviors: we understand that for Brandom the danger is to be able to believe that the study of the regularity of behaviors could alone make it possible to determine the presence of norms and this without taking into account the question of what the agents themselves had in mind within the framework of these same regular behaviors).[41]

Regulism and *regularism* are finally only a declination of the – now classical – conception of rules in Searle, which itself opposes constitutive rules and normative rules. The latter correspond to regularities and are endowed with a prescriptive scope: they are the codification of a situation to which they add nothing. The former are standardised and internalised rituals: they are an analytical form. It is understood that adherence to these theses implies adherence to a community or institutional conception of language.

Escaping from these two pitfalls, he will try to solve the question posed from the study of sanctions from a holistic perspective. In this sense, he will have to analyze the legal status of sanctions. He will thus consider that the latter can be considered as giving rise to changes in "normative status."

> The evaluative response constituting the community's recognition of such a norm … can, in some cases, be described in non-normative terms – the person who violates the norm is beaten with sticks, the behavior violating the norm is negatively sanctioned. But other cases are possible, for example, those in which the evaluative response is to punish by making other actions inappropriate – the person who violates the norm is not allowed to attend the weekly festival. In such a case, the normative meaning of the transgression is itself specified in normative terms (what is appropriate, what the transgressor is entitled to do).[42]

Brandom, in this analysis, refers to the existence of two types of sanctions. On the one hand, internal sanctions and, on the other hand, external sanctions. According to him, a normative system can perfectly well have only internal sanctions (a practice can thus be "all in norms"). Naturally, such a system remains largely improbable, since it would be based on compliance with sanctions, without anything being able to compel compliance with them from the outside. What Brandom expresses in this presentation is that internal sanctions do not *logically* need to be founded in the presence of external sanctions. This formulation allows him to demonstrate the presence of a rule that would be *implicit* and that favors the respect of internal sanctions: a practice would potentially be, according to his formula, "all in norms."

second-order standards to be enforced?" See J. HEATH, "Brandom and the Sources of Normativity," *Philosophiques*, 28 (1) (2001), p. 29.

41 It is easy to understand that in this case there will simply be too many rules that will appear to be coherent with regard to the concrete case that will be the object of the examination.

42 *Cf.* R. BRANDOM, *Rendre explicite*, *op. cit.* p. 126. In this sense, it distinguishes between internal and external sanctions.

What seems important in this analysis resides in the fact that Brandom's study tends to move away from a "naturalist" approach in favor of an expressivist[43] approach.

It should be understood that, from a naturalistic perspective, an approach oriented towards a search for the truth of the statements will be favored. For Brandom (who appears, in this sense, as an anti-naturalistic), it is possible to consider normativity in terms not of random modalities but of deontic modalities. From then on, he notes that these deontic modalities form, specifically, an expressive vocabulary: we speak and we use these words in order to speak. There is thus, obviously, an obvious primacy of the prescriptive over the descriptive in Brandom's thought, and of expression over description. We do not base the normativity of the concept in a relation to the world or in a certain perception of causality, but in the fact (very simple and very obvious) that we speak and we exchange in the framework of a certain market the reasons for the arguments that make our normative status evolve:

> Brandom's characteristic will be to extend this type of pragmatic and inferential conception to the content of the proposals. Let's show it by a trivial example: suppose that, lazily slumped in the deckchair of a farmhouse in the Camargue, I suddenly hear my interlocutor declare: "There is a bull in the living room"; I will infer from this a certain number of propositions (or beliefs) such as the bull is not a placid animal; there is therefore a danger; I must therefore be careful and consequently act by calling the firemen or feverishly complying with a bullfighting manual, but in any case by taking a certain number of actions. I attribute these inferences to my interlocutor and if by any chance he were to reject them all, astonished by my sudden panic, I would conclude that his concept of bull has no conceptual content here.[44]

Normativity as a concept is thus linked, in the same sense, to the sharing of a world and a certain rationality: a system of beliefs involved in a specific structure of expressiveness. Expressivity would not, in this perspective, be the capacity to

43 The act of language implies in terms of conceptual inferences: it implies new propositions of new beliefs. These different inferences I will attribute to the speaker and, if the speaker rejects them, I will then deduce that his concept has no conceptual content. We can see that in this perspective I do not need to study its representation or examine its mental image: meaning is linked to a system of inferences.

44 I. THOMAS-FOGIEL, "Présentation," in R. BRANDOM, *Rendre explicite, op. cit*, p. 22 This question of implicitness is also rooted in contextualist approaches which distinguish various levels of meaning: a linguistic meaning (which is non-contextual, in this purely semantic meaning the potential content is somehow encoded by the words, the utterance is reflexive: the literal content is given by the very rule of language); then there is a contextual content, the meaning is actualised by the context; finally there is a purely pragmatic meaning according to which the meaning is communicated by the utterance. This last approach is inferentialist: it is a question of perceiving not only what the sentence says, but what the speaker wants to say by enunciating the sentence: the expressed intention.

manifest externally something that previously was internal, but the capacity to make appear as explicit "something" that previously was implicit. It is a question of transforming a "doing" into a "saying." What the concept expresses is a specific "doing."

This analysis is not ignored by contemporary philosophy. An author like Goodman[45] who presents himself as unrealistic thus believes that symbols describe reality less than they produce it. For him, therefore, there is an ontological pluralism inherent in the fact that reality exists only in language. There is a dependence of the world on language. This ontological pluralism is realistically elaborated from a dispositional realism that seems to be able to be declined in the legal framework and to offer the key to the interpretation of normativity itself. In this perspective, legal concepts are only the actualization of the relationships between provisions: actualizations of the various deontic modalities that exist.

II A realistic implementation of the concepts of disposition in law

Claudine Tiercelin in the elaboration of her "dispositional realism" seeks to demonstrate that our reality, in its use of dispositions, offers them to manifest themselves according to properties that things possess "in power." It should be understood that this possibility of being is fully, within this framework, a reality and a true action. Is it not the very nature of the law for example, to be thus a promise to[46] be and to be, however, the bearer of real effects? In the same way that the fragility of glass is real, the normativity of a promise would be real. If the fragility of the glass (its disposition) actualises itself in contact with another object with which it is in contact, it is possible to envisage that the norm as a concept actualises its disposition in a specific context. These provisions, it should be remembered, are thus real. It is enough, according to the example often developed by Tiercelin, to remember the very concrete care we take to put away a crystal glass to understand this reality of fragility and its social effects.

This question intersects with the law with regard to the examination of an ontology of the normative. It seems to us that this dispositional realism developed by the philosopher offers to complete two essential legal intuitions: the first relating to the nature of the norm and the second to the effects of normativity. Law would be a field in which the norm actualises a real agreement between a *noem* and a *status* (A) and normativity would be our disposition to accept a natural form of rationality (B).

A The norm as a natural meeting between a noème and a status

According to a classical analysis that seems to me to sum up perfectly the state of legal science, it is possible to apprehend this concept of norm according to a typology that could be the following and that has been set out by Professor A.

45 N. GOODMAN, *Manières de faire des mondes*, Gallimard, Paris, 2006.
46 P. DI LUCIA, *L'universale della promessa*, Giuffrè, Milan, 1997.

Tale.[47] It is understandably an attempt to clarify the ambiguity surrounding the use of this term.[48]

A norm can thus appear in the jurist's discourse in five different forms: a deontic statement, a deontic proposition, a deontic enunciation (these first three forms seem to be linked to the inscription of law in language and thus inscribe the concept of norm in a conceptual cluster associating reference, deference, inference, connotation, etc.). In a more transgressive way, Professor Conte also believes that the norm is likely to appear as sometimes disengaged or disenclosed from language and then manifest itself as a deontic state of affairs. What is then presented is a *noème* in action in the world or in reality. This noeme is also likely to appear only in the mind, so we will speak in the language of Professor Tale of deontic noeme (it will be understood in a certain way as inert, because it is inherent in thought and not present in the world of action).

The concept of disposition and the elaboration of a disposition realism are likely to explain and develop this first intuition. Indeed, the *noème* would account for the causal dynamics wich in the social world take the form of normativity. The disposition of this *noème* would be to provoke a deontic state of affairs. A relationship between things that could be actualised and thus make the norm visible. This situation, which thus places the norm in the world and not only in language, could give consistency to certain analyses that deal with a silent law. The most eminent examples of these questions can be found in the famous Italian comparativeist R. Sacco[49] with the emergence of his concept of crypto-types and in the sociologist Th. Geiger.[50]

It is understandable that from this perspective the world is not made of independent substances, but of relations understood in the form of dispositions. It is then a certain way of giving reason to Leibnitz more than to Descartes.

It appears from this perspective that standards exist and that they are normative. They are part of a rational belief system. If we did not assume a certain rationality of behavior in this way, we could not interpret behavior as being regulated. There is, as we presented earlier, an application of the principle of charity as worked out by Davidson. Norms are not reduced to provisions that would be inherent in our nature. They are an imperative and can only work that way because they are based on the values that accompany the process of their development. They develop into a "life form" that agrees on this criterion of rationality. This approach is significantly different from the communicational rationality developed by some: it is not a question of being socially set in motion

47 A.G. CONTE, "Norms: 'Cinque referenti'." For a French translation of this text: L. PASSERINI GLAZEL and P. RICHARD, eds., *Philosophie du language normatif: anthologie de textes du professeur A.G. Conte*, Laval, Quebec, 2020.

48 On the philosophy of the norm: the remarkable work, G. LORINI and L. PASSERINI GLAZEL, eds., *Filosofie della norma*, Giappichelli, Turin, 2012.

49 On this question: L. PASSERINI GLAZEL, *Act norm type*, "Descriptare e cryptotipi," *op. cit.*, pp. 227–236.

50 For an introduction to the sociology of Th. Geiger, A.G. CONTE, *Sociologia filosofica del diritto*, Giappichelli, Turin, 2011.

Table 5.1 References of legal statements: synthesis of theoretical approaches

The term standard refers to five different deontic species.	Language Entities	The deontic statement: Consideration of the context of the statement: literal interpretation of the standard. The deontic proposal In the context of semantics: proposition is not synonymous with statement. The proposition is a semantic entity: it is the meaning of an utterance, i.e., what the utterance expresses. The deontic enunciation: A deontic enunciation is the enunciation of a statement that generates a deontic "state of affairs" that the statement is concerned about.	It is not possible to predict a violation, transgression or circumvention of these linguistic entities.
	A deontic state of affairs	The deontic status: a deontic state of affairs Some utterances produce deontic status But not all deontic statuses are generated by deontic enunciations (e.g., a legislative act).	Rodolfo Sacco and Theodor Geiger challenge the linguistic nature of the standards.[51]
	The deontic *noème*: A deontic noeme is the objective aspect of a deontic *noesi*. These two terms *Noema* (from Greek νόήμα) and *Noesis* (from Greek νόήσις) are technical terms that come from the phenomenology of Edmund Husserl.	Difference with the deontic proposal: The deontic noeme is an *intentional* entity (an intentional object of thought) whereas the deontic proposition is an *intentional* entity (in the sense of understanding). Difference with a deontic status: A *noème* is a *status* in thought Whereas a *status* is a *noème* in action.	

by values (those that would have been released from communicational rationality), but of being the embodiment of values that exist only through the "form of life" in which we agree.[52]

B Normativity as the disposition of the individual as an ethical animal

With regard to normativity, the question of provisions overlaps with the legal analysis based on what some legal sociologists understand as *nomotropism*. This involves examining the way in which the behavior of individuals turns or is oriented

52 In our opinion, this is a powerful connecting point, for example, between C. Tiercelin's reading of Peirce's work and S. Cavell's analyses of the nature of the life form.

itself according to the presence of legal rules. Not simply as the application of a norm, but also based on the very existence of these norms. Professor Conte[53] highlighted three paradoxes linked to nomotropism. The first is that acting according to the norm does not necessarily imply that the legal norm can be fulfilled [when, for example, the fulfilment of the rule results from the behavior of someone other than oneself], the second results from the presence of a norm that implies a behavior or is articulated with a behavior that is likely to generate two different actions, and the third seems to indicate that nomotropic behavior may be ***abducible*** in[54] Peirce's sense.

A proper understanding of abduction in the pragmatist's thinking seems to be understood not so much as a process of inventing hypotheses, but as the recognition that a hypothesis may appear to be a worthy candidate for further examination. From this perspective, abduction can always be seen as part of the context of discovery. It would act as a selection filter, allowing certain hypotheses to move to the next stage, thus allowing them to be subjected to empirical testing. The selection criterion is that there must be a reason to suspect that the hypothesis is true. We will have such a reason if the hypothesis implies that the observed facts we wish to explain are self-evident. This would indeed give better meaning to Peirce's assertion that abduction is a logical operation.

Nomotropism, which conceptually seeks to explain how social behavior is oriented according to the presence of a norm, manifests the embodiment of a certain natural rationality in a form of life.

It is this embodiment – and this agreement – in the form of life that explains the normativity, that is, the effectiveness [in the German sense] of the norm.[55]

> A background of exhaustive and systematic chords, without our realizing it (or not being aware of it). Wittgenstein gives these chords sometimes the name of conventions, sometimes that of rules.... Wittgenstein calls agreement in judgments (§ 242) the agreement on the basis of which we act, and our ability to use language depends, according to him, on agreement in forms of life (§ 241). Now forms of life are precisely, according to him, what must be accepted; for they are given.[56]

There is an immediate confidence of man in the effective norm and this can be explained phenomenologically by a correspondence between status and *noème*. The challenge is therefore to be aware of this correspondence and of a certain sense of rationality. It is the certainty and peace in the application of the norm that demonstrates the rationality of a behavior: the affirmation of a certain happiness in the end.

53 "Nomotropism," in A.G. CONTE, *Sociologia filosofica del diritto*, Giappichelli, Turin, 2011, pp. 47–55.

54 *The Collected Papers of Charles Sanders Peirce*, vols 1–6: C. HARTSHORNE and P. WEISS, eds, Harvard University Press, Cambridge, MA, 1931–1935; vols 7–8: A.W. BURKS, ed., Harvard University Press, Cambridge, MA, 1958.

55 It is a matter of referring here to *Wirklichkeit in* the sense of actual reality.

56 S. CAVELL (1979), *The claim of reason,* Oxford University Press, New York, 1979.

It should be noted that this certainty is built from the criteria. These do not so much provide us with certainty about the reality of a thing as they allow us to identify what that thing is in order to better "find our way" with certainty.

> By using criteria, we are not trying to explain, or prove the fact that we have agreed among ourselves in words (and therefore in life forms). One only describes the same fact in another way; or rather, there is a possible recourse when agreement is threatened, or lost. We use formal criteria when value judgments have to be made; but we use Wittgenstein's criteria when "we don't know where we stand," when we are lost in relation to our words, and the world they anticipate. We then seek to find ourselves again by discovering and declaring the criteria on which we agree.[57]

It is the peaceful practice of ordinary law which thus offers us a basis for our certainty and the effectiveness of law and rule. Relying on the feeling of certainty and peace is thus far from being as irrational as it may seem, it is even paradoxically the most certain and assured manifestation of rationality. In a form of life, it is our whole being that forms the basis of a practice. The appeased feeling that is expressed in the rational acceptance of legal belief is called by logic itself and presents itself as a sign of wisdom seated in the world and in action. It is the very manifestation of nature and the rule of evolution: a naturalism in the use of reason. We are ethical animals, to use a formula of Tiercelin.[58]

It is thus appropriate to adhere to the singular manner that Putnam[59] develops when he reworks the concept of reason. For him the latter is substantial and immanent in that it is factual and particular, whereas it is formal and transcendent in that it is universal and princely. Indeed, the world has an immediate reality, but exists for us only in concrete language games and in a form of life. Regularities are grammatical, but regular phenomena exist. Whitin this framework reason is immanent, because it cannot be found outside institutions and concrete games, but it is also transcendental, because it appears as a regulating idea offering us to criticise institutions and actions.

Normative normativity would then be faithful to what Wittgenstein states in paragraph 242 of his text Of *Certainty:* "Do we not have to say at every step: 'I believe it with certainty'?"

57 S. CAVELL, *Les voix de la raison, op. cit.*, p. 71.

58 Expression used by C. Tiercelin in his seminar conducted at the Collège de France as part of the Metaphysics and Philosophy of Science Chair between 2011 and 2012 on dispositions. In this case on March 21, 2012 on ethical provisions.

59 H. PUTNAM, *Definitions: Why can't reason be naturalized*, L'éclat, Paris, 1992.

6 The impossible experience of rapport in the work of Professor A. Conte...

The work of Professor A.G. Conte is one of the most fascinating and intriguing. Yet paradoxically (and because of its logical form) everything is already there before our very eyes. It manifests an evanescent event that always seems to come back. It illustrates, in its own singular way, a *monstration* that is inherent in the impasses of the capacity of expression of a thought through language.

Beyond the questions posed and apprehended by Professor Conte (the nature of norm or validity, the influence of performativity on legal language, the necessary clarification of certain syntagms used in legal statements) the fascination results, in our opinion, from the very nature of the object around which the work of the philosopher and jurist from Pavia seems to revolve. There is thus in this work a melancholy that seems unimpeachable in the works of the philosopher and logician. We know, of course, the distinction that must be made between these two terms: melancholy is a mental state that refers to the actual loss of an object; while nostalgia is the ability to remember that lost object. Melancholy is, in this way, a reflexivity (or an awareness) of nostalgia: it is about taking the object for what it really is (that is, that "nothing" that always escapes the language and translation of a thought). The only viable solution then being finally to show it.

There is thus in this work a "melancholic labyrinth" whose logic is complicated, at the time of the first confrontation, to understand. The technicality, the assumed redundancy, the sought-after bifurcations, the inferences, the mirrored approaches, form a framework that captivates and that must be apprehended in a subtle way. It is in a certain way "a movement of withdrawal" that offers us to think about an object by taking it away from us and from its ordinary use. Our intuition then resides in the fact that this work hides and reveals in the same movement.[1] The knowledge expressed by Professor Conte is expressed, in this way, in the form of anamorphosis. To shed light on the use of this structure, it seems possible to refer to Lévi-Strauss. In his famous text on dualistic organizations,[2] the French

1 A.G. CONTE, "*La brume cache des lieux et révèle des espaces*," in *Kenningar*, Adriatica, Bari, 2006. The logical form of the analysis is like a mirror that could play the role of limit.

2 C. LÉVI-STRAUSS, "Les organisations dualiste existent-elles?" in *Anthropologie structurale*, Plon, Paris, 1985. Chapter 2, "This is not the first time that research has brought us face to face with institutional forms that could be called type zero. True sociological antiprotons, they would have no intrinsic property other than to introduce the

DOI: 10.4324/9781003130109-7

anthropologist had emphasised the presence of an antagonism that the inhabitants of the village of Winnebagos in the "Great Lakes" region would be incapable of presenting. The symbolic structures would thus be elaborated in a dualistic form. They would express two attempts to account for an identical and impassable failure. It is understandable that this is not a trivial matter of reporting a kind of cultural relativism, but of reporting a common reference that is unthinkable. Language, logic, and culture itself are presented as causes to things (but causes that are paradoxically generated by their own effects). This is a question that pragmatism has perfectly grasped: language, logic, rationality are only normative beliefs that appear to be stabilised within a reality. They are capable of resisting the shocks of certain argumentation and of readjusting themselves to the periphery with respect to the experiences of the world. We recognise here what some present as conditions of guaranteed assertability.

The relationship that is established between language, thought, and the world is not of a "correlationist" nature. In this sense, thought is not an access to the thing, but the specific way (inherent in various contexts: "formats," "states of things," "forms of life") to think a thing as it is apprehended in a certain way and then to normalise it from its very contingency. What is thus real is not a reference (any transcendence with regard to the meaning of the thing), but the reality and relevance of the enunciation in the world. It is the enunciation that will normativeise the context of the enunciation in order to be able to account for its truth and for what is important with regard to the relevance of the enunciation.[3]

This failure is then itself "represented" (made present) in the symbolic order: language, logic, law, etc., in the symbolic order. This "zero type" institution – as Lévi-Strauss calls it – expresses a negative function for the benefit of a whole. This is perhaps an illustration of those antinomies that have been understood since Kant as inherent in reason itself. To mask this antinomy, an institution would be retroactively "naturalised" by the very emergence of a symbolic and cultural order. From then on, it naturalises the meaning it arouses. This meaning will then be likely to found various developments: the institution will thus generate causes where only reasons exist at best.

This intuition seems to us to be developed by Conte, in the legal field, under two aspects: in the logical form of his scientific discourse and in the aesthetic form of his pictorial or poetic creation.

These two facets enlighten each other – and dialectically – and testify to the inscription, at the heart of Professor de Pavia's thinking, of a difference that reveals the constitutive flaws of thought (in the form of a kind of "type zero" institution). The latter has no "in itself" meaning, but rather testifies to the constitutive "trait" of the institution. This trait that we find, for example, in Wittgenstein's analyses with the concept of "family likeness" and which forms the basis of the inscription of an identity. The result, in our view, is presented under three aspects: that of the "empty place"

preconditions for the existence of the social system to which they belong, to which their presence – in itself devoid of meaning – makes it possible to pose as a totality."

3 On this question: J. BENOIST, *L'adresse du réel*, Vrin, Paris, 2017.

that forms the basis of the logical space it organises; that of an *image* that, in a certain way, makes this space subjective; that of a *word that* expresses the real gap between what is stated and the subject that poses the enunciation. Finally, it is a question of referring to these three dimensions of analysis that Professor Conte was fond of in his work: syntax (I), semantics (II) and pragmatics (III).

I Logic as a necessary expression of thought: syntax

With Professor Conte, a "grammar" of extreme logical rigor is developed, which imposes its own necessity and demonstrates, in this way, what necessity itself is (for language and thought). The various research projects of the philosopher of Pavia concerning: the examination (or analycity) of "normativity"; the study of "validity"; the examination of the effectiveness of norms, etc. testify to this reflection. It is a question, finally, of trying to understand how the *deontic is* elaborated; how it is thus possible to make the world and the discourse (which develops at the heart of it) go together without being trapped by metaphysics.

One aspect of Conte's thought seems to me, in this respect, particularly enlightening. In the last book of a series of books that compiles almost all of his work, the Italian researcher sets out, in a long introduction, what seems to him to be the essence of his thinking at the time.

He then set out to explain a maritime metaphor: "the dead work."[4] We know that in the lexical field that is peculiar to nautical art, "dead works" are distinguished from "living works," which are the parts of the ship that are submerged and thus located below the waterline.

Here we find the taste for dichotomies that is essential in the analytics of Conte. Two types of works, two different fields, two places that reactivate opposition and difference and construct the idea of a distinction and an articulation between these places and spaces, are thus opposed. This willingness to back up one's reflection with mirror games or a dichotomous approach to a question is important (it is classic in Conte's analyses). In our opinion, it testifies to a certain perception of the social world. The two elements that are thus opposed never really relate to each other: they testify, in fact, to a perception of difference that should be emphasised.

They do not form, truly, a prior unity – which could only be imaginary. They bear witness to an unalterable difference that is more radical: what is thus "real" is this "feature"[5] of difference (which is inherent to a system and its syntax) – just as

4 A.G. Conte, "Opera morta: tre temi emergenti," in *Filosofia del linguaggio normativo,* Giappichelli, Turin, 2001, pp. 25–43. This intuition seems to us to be reinforced by what Professor Conte himself declares of Wittgenstein in his text "Wittgenstein non postumo," in A.G. Conte, ed., *L. Wittgenstein, Tractatus logico-philosophicus e altri scritti filosofici non postumi,* Einaudi, Torino, 1989, pp. 7–18. In this text he considers the Tractatus to be Wittgenstein's dead work and he begins his analysis with the following enigma: "Πλέον ημισυ παντός [*la metà è piu del tutto*]."

5 This "trait" is "what matters" for the question that the standard is supposed to answer. It is the standard's openness to what it is relevantly capable of measuring as a cognitive anchor in the reality of its enunciation.

a letter is distinguished, for example, from another by the presence of a simple pencil stroke in an alphabet: think of the difference between "p" and "b."

There are two different conceptions of our capacity to make the unity of a thing or a category of things. The latter can be understood either as an *a priori* category or as the sum of certain things. In the first hypothesis, the category is understood abstractly and its understanding is determined beforehand. In the second hypothesis, the category is understood as an open classification which is never more than the sum of things that can be developed. The first hypothesis involves the inferential play of cause and effect, while the second hypothesis generates *reasons* that are never merely *a posteriori* justifications. In this sense, the oppositions constructed by logical thought do not relate to each other and reflect the fact that thought is only a way of giving meaning to the world (in a given syntax) and that it is not intended to describe it as it is. Here is an ultime mirage to be deciphered and discarded: language, like thought, is not a mirror – if not, as Conte wrote, a "silent mirror" – but an ever-unique way of weaving our relationship to the world *into* the world and in the language it generates.

It is this shift – and this movement of difference – that is constantly questioned by Conte.[6] The "dead work" represents that part of the unthought that is irreducible and that we too often forget, since in order to make our symbolic system (political, legal, linguistic…) work, we make a fool of ourselves with words. There is there an "initial guilt" that must be assumed and that is instituted on the basis of a great and initial lie (*proton pseudos*). We know the legal effects of this widely accepted lie: thinking the law often renders it inapplicable.

The practitioner must apply the law as it is *given* as "positive law" and not *seek what* the law is. Thinking and applying are thus often antithetical. The universality of a reflection on law necessarily implies its non-existence. If "the law" exists, it can only be the expression of a certain local particularism: "a law." This relationship between the existence and the order of law seems essential for Conte: part of his reflections will thus tend to *reweave* the link between legal language and the world in which it develops. The Italian philosopher thus works to develop a phenomenology that takes into account certain predicative aspects without, however,

6 This situation could be related to a mathematical question related to the accessibility of real numbers. For Cantor and Gödel, this question of accessibility poses a problem with respect to the number 2. Gödel introduces this question of accessibility in an article on Cantor in 1947 ("What is Cantor's continuum problem?" in *Intuitionnisme et théorie de la démonstration*, Vrin, Paris, 2002). In his demonstration the accessibility of finite numbers starts at 3. There is thus a flaw in the generation of numbers that will present 2 as inaccessible by the sum of two numbers lower than itself. On this question, for example, J. LADRIÈRE, "Le rôle du théorème de Gödel dans le développement de la théorie de la démonstration," in *Revue philosophique de Louvain*, 1949, pp. 469–492. Also in a perspective of integrating this question into the psychoanalytical field (and specifically with regard to the Lacanian concept of *pastout*): M. BOUSSEYROUX, "Le pastout: sa logique et sa topologie," in *L'en-je Lacanien*, 2008/1 (10), pp. 9–27. "For finite numbers, accessibility does not begin until 3 … and continues for the whole integer sequence. There is thus a flaw in the generation of integers that makes 2 inaccessible by the sum of less than two numbers lower than 2."

getting lost in them. In other words, law does not seem to be a language endowed with purely conventional meaning.

II Eidograms supprimer as an illustration of logical space: semantics

Another key is offered to us in order to decipher the work of the Italian researcher. It is now a matter of referring to a facet of the philosopher that will not be directly developed in this work, but which nevertheless sheds light on various aspects of the professor's legal thought.

He was also an artist. It is appropriate here to focus on art as a technique (in its classical perception) and its assured function for the benefit of the development of thought. Professor Conte applied himself to create as an artist (or more precisely as a craftsman) would be likely to do. He applied a technique to *show something of* the world that he was trying to *present* (to make present) to the thinking of others. His graphic creations (these are *eidograms* according to Professor Conte[7]) admirably testify to this desire, even beyond the technique used and the assumed refusal to use the tools offered by our ultra-modernity. These graphic creations, which are scattered throughout Professor Conte's work, represent a proliferation of statements that will be integrated into piles of geometric forms (through reflexive games or by the implementation of anamorphoses).

These arrangements bring the identical repetition of certain cultural objects to a certain *climax*.

In the – natural – movement of interpellation that language and culture impose on us, there is always a "remnant" which, to use the famous formula, never blooms. With these graphic games, the layout will be distorted. Professor Conte thus makes the order of symbolic representation *wince*. What the graphic facet of Professor Conte's work shows is, in our opinion, a reiteration of his logical demonstration.

To some, this could manifest a certain monstrosity: it appears to us as revealing a sublime activity. Naturally, the sublime must then be apprehended under a specific register and as the fact of raising the object that we show (under a certain appearance) to the level of what always escapes representation.[8] It is the expressiveness of this difference between the object and the thing that expresses the sublime of the effort of thought. Professor Conte is then of total and absolute authenticity he *shows the* place where the necessity of his thought is elaborated. Rare are the authors who are so sincere about the premises of their analyses and who thus manifest the place where the truth and the lie inherent in all discourses are held.

It is also a question of shedding a different light on the idea of "dead work," the importance we have already pointed out. The translation – and

7 By this neologism, Professor Conte linked in a representation on the one hand an *Eidos* (an idea, a form) and the inscription of a line.

8 In this anamorphic creation something falls before our eyes and appears as a silent cry.

highlighting – of these "dead works" seems to have been one of the driving forces behind the Italian professor. This work is only dead in the order of law (of which it is the unthought). The "dead work" changes its nature, however, when one accepts the idea that law itself is necessarily *in* life – *in* "a form of life." What is real is this gap inherent in our interpellation by language between life and the words that derive from it: and this even in the order of law.

III Poetry as pragmatic of the logical space

Conte's scientific work is complex and exotic. However, it has a charm and strength that is difficult to deny. Beyond the neologisms and the formidable erudition, there is a "*je ne sais quoi*" that commands attention.

It is not really – or not only – the fact that the logical form inherent in the analysis masks a phenomenon,[9] which would be inaccessible: the "legal phenomenon" in itself or the "reference" of language (and more specifically of legal language as a specialised language), etc.

It is obvious that natural – or formal – language always participates in the construction of reality and that the denotation relationship is more complex than it appears *a priori* (and that it should be more judiciously approached under the aspects specific to the relationship between *Sinn* and *Bedeutung*).

It is not, as we shall see, that language relates to a real or is deduced from it: it is, finally, that language develops as an enunciation within it.

There is a dichotomy here that we must be careful not to get caught up in. Language (like all human practices) is woven *into* the world and is not overshadowed by it. In this sense, the same applies to the commandment that *is* in the world. This is expressed in the logical form as used by the Italian philosopher.

With A.G. Conte, the discourse on law clearly manifests its lack. It integrates the impasse that finally constitutes it and offers us this incredible gift thanks to which it is possible to place in full light certain lies, certain weaknesses of thought or certain blunders that are proper to the expressiveness of our thinking.

Professor Conte's recurrent use of this differentiation between the registers of semantics, syntax and a pragmatic approach to legal language testifies to the need to take seriously this discrepancy between "subject of utterance" and "subject of the enunciation." Ultimately, meaning always resides in our ability to question this discrepancy in a relevant manner.

In this perspective it should be noted that Professor Conte was also an artist in another aspect: he was a poet.[10] In this sense, he participated in a certain fabrication of the world through language. His purely scientific work is also, in our opinion, totally impregnated with this poetry. The use of a multiplicity of linguistic forms, the delightful construction of his neologisms, participate in this poetry that permeates his work and his research. In this sense, his attachment to "scaldic

9 A.G. CONTE, "*Phenomena. semblant without image, of an otherness that would only be semblant*," in *Kenningar*, *op. cit.*, 2006.

10 See A.G. CONTE, *Kenningar*, *op. cit.*, 2006.

poetry" appears to us as particularly significant. We know that this Scandinavian poetry is characterised, on the one hand, by a specific formal approach (a very great freedom offered in the arrangement of words that seems inherent to Old Norse) and, on the other hand, by a massive use of metaphors and periphrases.[11]

This final facet of Professor Conte's work seems to offer a final explanation of his work. The quest of the Italian philosopher and jurist seems to have been to question both "the lack of" who and what is proper to symbolic orders and "the lack in" inherent to these same symbolic orders (the various orders allowing the representation of a thing in their specific grammars: language, law, culture, etc.).

In this sense, the "lack of" presents itself, as we have seen, in the refusal to make law (or legal language) the mirror of the thing and access to the thing. The symbolic order thus participates in the creation of the reality to which it relates (the work inherent in research on constituent rules is, in this respect, particularly important). In a way, these "constitutive norms" anticipate what they concern: they express a retroactive performativity.

The "lack in," for its part, specifically concerns the lack of consistency of the symbolic order (which pragmatically cannot be satisfied with the idea that it could be constituted on the basis of an *exception*). It is this second approach that seems to express the poetic scope of Conte's work. In fact, the sum of these acts (statements and enunciations) is open to infinity and imposes in a continuous way a pragmatic rearrangement of one's own understanding.

Finally, this approach seems, intellectually speaking, quite close to the work of some American philosophers (we are thinking here, for example, of Stanley Cavell's analyses and his rereading of Wittgenstein's analyses on the question of "forms of life"). In this sense, "the lack of" appears to be the affirmation of an inherent deficiency in the "form of life" (or, more precisely, the taking into account of the necessary plurality of these forms of life, and thus of the "contextualism" of enunciation). The "lack in" refers, for its part, to the idea of a "whirlwind of life" and to the fact that life only catches up with its theoretical inconsistency in its own development. It is in this dialectic common to all symbolic orders (the dialectic of "lack of" and "lack in" or the dialectic of "form" and "life") that the ordinariness of a "form of life" is expressed.

This poetic form, prized by Professor Conte, was presented as "the first expression of a purely verbal jouissance" and this at the time "when the 'itinerant rhapsodes' were replaced by the *scaldes* who were poets animated by a few personal intentions." There is something here that seems to me exceptionally right. The poetry of Conte – like the whole of his work – testifies to this serene will to place life within life and to an identical (perfectly ethical) will to place this life within the very heart of "the life of words." The works that focus on the effectiveness of law

11 R. BOYER, "Scaldes et poésie scaldique" in *Enc. Univ.* 14. This poetry offers "a field of study virgin to current research, because it constitutes par excellence a language within a language and certainly represents the height of art that intends to give itself over while hiding, a pure intellectual and aesthetic enjoyment that does not however offend the pleasure of discovering once scratched the palimpsest of rich and warm personalities."

seem to us paradigmatic of this consideration: the normativity of legal discourse thus goes beyond the simple logical form of prescription.

Professor Conte is thus one of those who pushes thinking to its limits and pushes us to think. These works, published for the first time in French, should thus provide food for thought for jurists who are anxious to overcome certain sad habits peculiar to legal thought, certain aporias related to meanings held to be true by jurists that lead to dead ends and bad faith. The latter makes us accept, for convenience and cynicism sometimes, arguments that we feel are biased. A bad faith which, to paraphrase another poet, in total does not make us feel remorse, but an obscure embarrassment and which makes that when positive law is raised the jurist's coat drags a noise of dry illusions and regrets like a mourning dress drags dead leaves.

7 The ordinariness of a political commitment and its normativities

With this text, the aim is to apprehend the relationship that is established between the subjective and objective perspectives inherent in a *democratic* political relationship. In this sense, it will be appropriate to do justice to a policy with a "human face" to paraphrase the formulas of A. Dubcek[1] and H. Putman.[2] The objective is important and aims at a reconciliation of two unimpeachable dimensions of our democratic "form of life" (the life we live *with* our concepts and that develops with regard to the relevance of these concepts). These seem not only irreconcilable, but at the basis of our unfortunate consciousness. As such, it seems more and more obvious that what we need in the field of political philosophy and the analysis of its normativities is *descriptions and* a certain *sense of the* obvious.[3] The most difficult thing would then be to hear beyond the discourses of our specialised languages (politics, law, etc.). We have, in a way, become deaf because of the noise generated by our ideologies. The expressions usually used are ambiguous. They express a misunderstanding and, above all, an *agreement* on this misunderstanding. The latter is rooted in a feeling that reflects too ordinary an obviousness. There is in our daily presence in the world a form of synaesthesia that hinders the obviousness (the obviousness) of what we live. What is currently so difficult to hear it is still possible to see or feel, in the face of this singular presence in the world, a feeling of obviousness.

An epistemological problem should initially be ruled out. The "grammar" that commands our relationship to the world (and organises it) is naturally incapable of analyzing itself. However, it is still possible, according to the famous formula, to show it. The first step in this quest for the ordinary of a political relationship therefore probably lies in resistance to ideology.

What characterises the latter is its invisibility or transparency. Indeed, as soon as it organises our relationship to the world, it presents itself as the blind spot that is inherent to social perception. With ideology there is an erasing of what does not

1 To quote his program reporting on socialism with a human face in 1968.

2 H. PUTNAM, *Le réalisme à visage humain*, Gallimard, Paris, 2011.

3 The theory of description as presented by Russell is a theory of denotation. It focuses on the logical form of expressions and manifests the ambiguity of some of our expressions with respect to what they denote.

DOI: 10.4324/9781003130109-8

function in accordance with it and of what escapes the norm that it generates. Our dominant ideology imposes, in the political field, a specific vision of the individual that can be subject to a certain deconstruction. This deconstruction seems to us to be offered by linking two classical reflections on man that were initiated by Althusser and Gramsci (I). These descriptions seem to open the door to a pragmatic and realistic critical analysis of the inscription of man in the various normativities. These elaborate his ordinariness and differ from his presence as subject of law and subject of law. As such, the subject would be only one voice (II).

I A subject erased *in* and *by* ideology

A struggle against ideology often pays for itself with a pound of flesh. To illustrate this facet, we will call upon one of the philosophers who lived through this resistance and struggle painfully. He is a Hegelian Marxist: Gramsci and his conception of man *as* history. In front of him we will develop a structuralist vision of the inscription of the individual in politics (the individual being reduced to a disembodied place inherent in the game of a social structure). The issue at stake between these two theses seems to be the following: is the person a subject (A) or is the subject no one (B)? Is the social relation elaborated on the basis of inscriptions in normativities that never totally exhaust the person, or on the contrary, is the person inscribed in his or her relations ultimately only an epiphenomenon – and an effect of these – that is to say, an effect of these relations?

A The person as subject

The conception of the individual in the philosopher *d'Ales*[4] is based on a philosophy of *praxis*[5] perceived as an anthropology.[6] According to this, man *is* history. In this sense, Gramsci's political thought (as well as constitutional ideas) seems to show a certain mistrust of both precise institutional formulas and mechanisms for ensuring the balance of power.[7]

It is possible to find traces of this specific perception of the human in the text of the Transalpine Republican Charter. It is now well known that the elaboration of the Italian Constitutional Charter was mainly under the influence, on the one hand, of the social doctrine of the church and, on the other hand, of socialist

4 Antonio Gramsci was born in Ales near Cagliari in Sardinia on January 22 1891. On the life of the Sardinian philosopher see the biography of S.F. ROMANO, *Gramsci*, UTET, "La vita sociale della nuova italia," 8, 1965, p. 400.

5 Some believe that Gramsci used this expression of philosophy of praxis only to deceive the vigilance of the prison censors. This expression should be understood as a mask applied to the idea of dialectical materialism. This view seems somewhat reductive with respect to the autonomy that this notion seems to assume in Gramsci's work.

6 A.-R. BUZZI, *La théorie politique d'Antonio Gramsci*, Nauwelaerts, Louvain, 1967, p. 163 ff.

7 "Today a cop is worth more than a deputy; the cop is an element of power, the deputy is a legal fiction," in *Les écrits politiques, Avanti*! June 1, 1919, I, 1914–1920, Gallimard, Paris, 1974, p. 237.

ideas. Thus, "Christian personalism" and Marxism are intimately linked to the elaboration of this text[8] as the expression of a common perception conveying a humanism to which these great political formations are attached.[9] The Italian left thus preferred to attach to its name the authorship of the programmatic elements of the constitutional text to the detriment of institutional analyses.[10]

The programmatic principles defended by the Italian left can be usefully classified into two categories.[11] On the one hand, statements such as that conveyed by

8 Prior to the adoption of the constitutional text, the only leftist party that presented itself as the bearer of a genuine reform project was the *Partito d'azione* (its political program was oriented towards the establishment of a presidential regime of rigid separation of powers – the head of state could appoint and dismiss ministers, legislative delegations to the government were forbidden). It is clear that the other formations of the Italian left, however, were not without ideals to defend. These ideals were, in the beginning, a decisive part of the new republican charter. Historically, the work of the Constituent Assembly was preceded by that of various commissions set up by the Minister for the Constitution. The collegial nature of these formations makes it difficult to determine what share is due to members of left-wing formations and thus poses a real problem of interpretation. However, it would seem that the main lines concerning the form of the state, the rights to be guaranteed to individuals and the necessarily rigid nature of the Constitution are not clear. There was a certain consensus among political formations on both the left and the right. On the contrary, the elements of dissension appear in all their clarity (and this time in a way that is easy to distinguish because the discussions were published) during the debates in the Constituent Assembly, which will take place in two phases. In the first phase, from July 20, 1946 to February 1, 1947, the draft Constitution is drawn up by the *Constitutional Commission* (it has become common to call this Commission "Commission of 75" in accordance with the number of its members. This body is itself divided into three sub-commissions.). In a second stage, the draft Constitution will be examined by the Assembly in plenary session.

9 It is possible to highlight an inspiration common to personalism and Marxism, since these philosophical currents are expressions of existentialism. *Cf.* J. LACROIX, *Marxisme, existentialisme personnalisme,* PUF, Paris, 1971. We voluntarily adopt a broad perception of the notion of existentialism. We are aware, in fact, of the criticisms leveled against this philosophical orientation by certain Marxist authors such as Georges Lukacs. "Thus, Sartre writes that what makes the fundamental project of human reality most conceivable is that man is the being who projects to be God… To be man is to tend to be God. This ideal of divinization of oneself means, translated into the language of philosophy: to attain the degree of being that ancient philosophy designated by the expression causa sui and which signifies the sovereign self-determination of being.… The Sartrean levelling of all manifestations of human existence resembles the deterministic conception except that, for determinism, these manifestations are inscribed in rationally constructed systems whereas in Sartre they are a priori deprived of all meaning. The Sartrean hypothesis of freedom empties freedom itself of all meaning." *Cf.*LUKACS, *Existentialism or Marxism,* Nagel, Paris, 1961, pp. 100–104.

10 This will is also found in the later practice of the Italian CP, which has always defended a global and systemic reading of the constitutional text. In the latter, the second part of the constitutional text had to be explained in the light of the principles set out in the first part.

11 The will of the Left to concentrate on the implementation of a political program was thus clearly realised when Togliatti observed in the Plenary Assembly of March 11, 1947, that if Stalin rejected the idea that the Constitution can be only a political

Article 3, paragraph 2, of the Constitution are affirmations of principle and will have to be transformed into reality by other provisions. On the other hand, the principles that present themselves, on the one hand, as a political orientation for the legislator and, on the other hand, as a limit to the possible intervention of the legislator.[12]

It seems to us, therefore, possible to perceive in the wording of some of these founding texts, and even more so in the *existentialist*[13] perception of man that they convey, the legacy of one of the most important proponents of Marxist ideology: Antonio Gramsci. Thus, the concepts of *person*,[14] the Italian perception of *decentralization* and *pluralism*,[15] as well as, for example, the protection of a some understanding of *culture*,[16] seem to us to be examined in this specific light.

Nevertheless, beyond this indirect institutional paternity, it appears that Gramsci's thought must rest, even before any institutional assembly has been implemented, on man's practical action. "The proletariat realizes its own order," he wrote in July 1918.[17] The heart of his political thought thus lies in the dialectical movement that is established between man and society. Dictatorship was thus described as capable, on its own, of allowing freedom. This vision is traditionally understood in Gramsci's work under the concept of hegemony. Derived from the Leninist concept of the "dictatorship of the proletariat," this notion is presented as the ability of the ruling class to make the rest of society adopt its values. The "ethical content of the state" is thus formed by this "cultural-political hegemony of a social group."[18] For Gramsci, this domination by the traditionally dominant

program, this analysis is valid only for a society in which the revolutionary process had already been accomplished. This is not, therefore, the case at present in Italy, where there is still a need to carry out social transformations that the constituents must identify and specify as necessary. "The Constitution thus resembles not a pact between the people and the sovereign to limit the arbitrariness of the latter and guarantee their rights, but a pact between the various political currents and social groups." For Togliatti, therefore, the constituents must act in order to transform society in accordance with the wishes of the people; it is in this that the substantial legitimacy of the constituents lies.

12 During this work, we can see that left-wing political formations found themselves in a situation that demonstrates how easily it has been possible to agree with the ideas put forward by some left-wing Catholics such as Fanfani or Taviani even on traditionally polemical issues such as those related to the economy.

13 Understood as a conscious commitment: "I hate the indifferent. I believe, like Friedrich Hebbel, that living means being partisan. One cannot just be a man who is a stranger to the city. Who really lives cannot but be a citizen and a partisan. Indifference is abhorred, parasitism, cowardice; it is not life. That's why I hate the indifferent." *Les écrits politiques,* I, 1914–1920, Gallimard, Paris, 1974, p. 102.

14 Gramsci's humanism manifests itself in the framework of a *catharsis* that develops according to a dialectic between consciousness and the world

15 Key concepts in Gramsci's perception of civil society.

16 Constitutionally protected. *Cf.* on this question the importance of ideology in Gramsci.

17 P. PETTA,*Ideologie costituzionali della sinistra italiana (1892–1974)*, Savelli, Rome, 1975, p. 67.

18 A. GRAMSCI, *Letters from the Prison* (1926–1937), letter 89, p. 178. www.uqac.uquebec.ca/zone30/Classiques_des_sciences_sociales/index.html

class is not democratic. It expresses only the continued exploitation of one social class. This hegemony is based on the notion of ideology, a central concept in Gramsci's analysis.

This conception of the world is the expression of a *truly* dialectical mechanism. According to Gramsci, one must be able to break down the notion of ideology in order to account for this dialectic. Thus, there are *historically organic ideologies* (those that historically organise the masses) and *arbitrary ideologies* (the only ones that can give rise to the seeds of polemics and be associated with error as an expression of selfishness). Ideology is thus the cement of the dominant social block.[19] From the moment Gramsci analyzes the notion of hegemony as a *critique*[20] that should allow the proletariat to return to itself and to represent itself as a "class for itself." In this sense, ideology becomes, at the same time, what maintains alienation and what can allow the proletariat to exercise its hegemony as an instrument of liberation.

This is sufficiently known that we are not allowed to develop it. This analysis therefore offers a specific place to the individual. *The intellectual*,[21] i.e., the man who becomes a philosopher (thus presenting himself as a true civil servant of superstructures) authorises the constitution of a *historical block*. Thus, in order to liberate himself, man must exercise a specific intellectual activity. He presents himself as a philosopher (for Gramsci, all men are intellectuals, but not all men are intellectuals in society). This program will be brought to its logical conclusion by means of a rejection of "man in general" and an approach that will privilege the links that exist between man and others on the one hand, and man and nature on the other.

Gramsci's conception of *umana personality* tends, in this way, to impose an abandonment of the individualistic image. The consciousness of individuals stages a relationship between oneself, others, and the world, and gives personality a function of rational direction. In this sense, "man's individuality resides in the totality of his relationships, to make oneself a personality means to acquire awareness of these relationships, to modify his personality means to modify one's relationships."[22] Revolution presupposes, therefore, a revolution *of* man which can only be made possible through a battle of ideas and polemics. In doing so, Gramsci challenges various postulates. He challenges philosophy that studies man without reference to the world and philosophies that deal with the world without reference to man.

19 H. PORTELLI, on Gramsci, in *Dictionnaire des œuvres politiques,* PUF, Paris, p. 355.

20 A. GRAMSCI, *Letters, op. cit.*, letter 89, p. 179.

21 It should be noted that, for our author, there would be intellectuals only in a relationship to politics.

22 A. GRAMSCI, *Letters, op. cit.*, letter 76, p. 159. In 1917, Gramsci was able to affirm that "socialists should not substitute an order for an order. They must establish order itself. The juridical maxim they want to realise is: the possibility of full realization of one's own human personality granted to all citizens." "La città futura," February 11, 1917. In *Les écrits politiques,* I, 1914–1920, Gallimard, Paris, 1974, p. 101.

This criticism, which stigmatises a philosophy in which man is absent, has for a long time made it possible to account for the structuralist current.[23] Beyond the long fragmented character of the transposition of Gramsci's work in France, it is therefore a *philosophical* obstacle that *ultimately* hindered the development of Gramsci's thought.[24] This thought thus stumbled over three pitfalls raised by the structuralists: the refusal to think of Marxism as philosophy, the rejection of Marxism as humanism, and finally the recusal of history itself.

B *The subject is no one*

For Althusser, for example, Marxism shares nothing with the ideological practices to which all philosophies can be reconducted:

> There is no theory on the one hand that would be a pure intellectual vision without body or materiality, and on the other hand an exclusively material practice.... This dichotomy is an ideological myth in which a theory of knowledge reflects many interests other than those of reason. (Cf. *Reading the Capital*).

This practice must be understood as the process of transforming a given material into a given product. This phenomenon of transformation is identified from then on in a specific *structure*.[25] For the structuralists, the past does not explain the present and the present does not carry the seeds of the future:

> Thus, in practice/theory there are neither subjects nor history. The real subjects of this practice are the objects of consciousness which must be explained by means of their internal. It is the very conception of any arrow of time that is thus called into question. It is the possibility of a history that is denied.[26]

Althusser's rereading of Marxism is thus clearly anti-historicism. Thus, the French philosopher was able to affirm in 1978: "Gramsci did not emerge from the Hegelio-Crocene conception of culture as the ultimate end of humanity, and therefore the ultimate stain on humanity.[27] This explains, for him, the sublimation of the state into hegemony operated by the Italian philosopher. In this way,

23 In the broadest sense, we know, indeed, what it is appropriate to think of the unity of such a movement since its founding fathers themselves refused this appellation. More precisely, we must speak of a structuralist method.

24 *Cf.* J. TEXIER, "Gramsci in Francia," in *Gramsci e la cultura contemporanea*, 2, Istituto Gramsci, Rome, 1975, p. 371 ff.

25 Perhaps the greatest merit of the structuralists is that they have made it possible to offer a theoretical model capable of resisting the opportunism of political practice and the fascination of a history abandoned to empirical data alone.

26 C. ZANCHETTIN, "L'epistemologia marxista di Louis Althusser," *Il Mulino*, 220, March–April, 1972, p. 261.

27 L. ALTHUSSER, *Philosophical and political writings*, Vol. 1, "Marx and his limits," Le livre de poche, Paris, 1994, p. 520.

Althusser operates an epistemological rereading[28] of Marx's work, allowing the highlighting of what "*shines by its absence*" *within* it. He brings to light a structure peculiar to Marxist discourse:

> In OTHER words, there is no subject at all, no center, no radiating nucleus, no living source or shadow mouth, but only decentralised mechanisms of mobile structures that slide one on top of the other, and whose only invariant feature is their formal law of variation.[29]

It should be noted that what allows a structure to *function in* this way is always[30] the existence of an empty box understood as *perpetuum mobile*.[31] For the French philosopher, this empty square, which is peculiar to Marxist discourse, lies in the existence of a meaningful absence:

> If it is true that it is to know how to hear in it what sounds hollow that a science progresses and lives, something of life and of the Marxist theory of history is perhaps suspended at this precise point where Marx, in a thousand ways, designates to us the presence of a concept essential to his own thought, but absent from his discourse.[32]

This blind point results from the absence of epistemological reflection in Marx (Althusser dates this epistemological break from 1845 and from *German ideology*). The opposition between Althusser and Gramsci is thus clear and crystallises in the refusal of history and in a refusal of humanism (for Gramsci, man makes history and, in doing so, he makes himself).

Yet can't this opposition be challenged? Structuralism leaves, in our opinion, room for *umana personality*. The law seems to us susceptible, despite its similarity to an ideological structure, to take the identification of the subject into its own hands. It is necessary, however, to return to the origins and foundations of law.

II A political subject *deferred* in ordinary normativities

The question now is therefore to determine whether the person is totally inscribed in the ideology or whether only one facet of it is likely to appear at the rhythm of

28 We understand by this term any coherent and critical discourse allowing to determine in a reasoned way and within a specific field of knowledge the different logics that inform knowledge or lack of knowledge.

29 J.-C. FORQUIN, "Lecture d'Althusser," in *Dialectique marxiste et pensée structurale, Les cahiers du Centre d'étude socialistes*, February–May 1968, p. 26.

30 Beyond the symbolic character of the structure itself – fundamental because of the neantilization it requires – and the importance of the topological representation of the relations generated by the structure.

31 Sort of blind spot that allows the series, which the structure distributes, to develop in the staging space offered by the structure. *Cf.* the well-known analysis of Edgar Poe's stolen letter.

32 L. ALTHUSSER and E. BALIBAR, *Lire le Capital*, 1, Maspero, Paris, 1968, p. 31.

normative social relations. We consider the part of the person that escapes his political inscription and the part that results from the place offered to the political "subject of enunciation." The deferred presence of the subject thus manifests itself in various places (A). It is in the continuous expression of this *difference* that pragmatism offers to discover the norms inherent in the rationality that governs the appearance of the subject (B).

A The places where the subject is updated

Thus we observe a *shift in the* classic concept of the subject. The structuralist (or poststructuralist) hero "is without identity, made up of non-personal individuations and pre-individual singularities."[33] The structure thus gives rise to a game in which places are not allocated to real beings, but are constantly updated, to the benefit of a subject who appears crumbled by the potentialities of the structure. The subject becomes nomadic,[34] he strips himself away by *differing.*

If Gramsci asserted that man is a process, and precisely the process of his acts (*Cf. M.S.*, p. 27), structuralism observes that the subject is the *being-subject of* a restricted world that is at the center only of its *renunciations* and *limits.*

Today's philosophy of law sometimes takes such a path within the framework of "a renewed foundation of law."[35] Within this foundation, contractualism needs to be reorganised.[36]

In Marxist thought, which is by principle anti-juridist, law is present in the field of power and contributes to the ideological reproduction of social relations as both a technique of domination and a means of spreading ideology. For Gramsci, ideology is an *implicit conception of the world* (it manifests itself in law as well as in art or economic activity) which makes it possible to clarify the concept of civil society (understood as a set of organs for the diffusion of ideology). For Louis Althusser, ideology is based not on a direct relationship to truth, but on the existence of presuppositions (it is an imaginary which is the product of personal histories) that reflect the real conditions of existence of individuals.[37] Althusser[38] thus highlights a *mise en abyme, a doubling, made possible by a mirror effect.* The imaginary relationship (Gramsci's conception of the world) presents itself as being *represented*: systematised. The motor of an ideology is therefore not, for him, to be sought in the ideology, but outside of it. In both cases, law is likely to be

33 G. DELEUZE, "What does structuralism MEAN?" in F. CHATELET, ed., *La philosophie au XX siècle*, Marabout, Paris, 4, p. 327.
34 According to the happy formula of Gilles Deleuze.
35 A. RENAUT and L. SOSOE,*Philosophie du droit,* PUF, Paris, 1991, p. 435.
36 K.O. Appel and J. Habermas can be included in this logic: the communication founds the subject, which reverses the classical paradigm.
37 C. ZANCHETTIN, "L'epistemologia marxista di Louis Althusser", *op. cit.*, p. 266.
38 It is curious to note that the day after the murder of his wife Louis Althusser declared: "I wanted to destroy myself at all costs because I have always been non-existent." This self-negation resonates as an astonishing echo of the death of man in one of the masters of structuralism.

presented, according to a now famous formula, as "the war itself" and "the strategy of that war in action." It is therefore up to legal science to redress this perspective.

Thus, man seems *ab initio* alienated from a symbolic structure[39] that needs to be dismantled. The law only redoubles this initial alienation through language. The subject thus undergoes a first and definitive renunciation.[40] A formative displacement of the subject appears. An *abstract fallacy* manifests itself. A symbolic fiction presides over the formation of the subject.[41] As a result, the subject must be understood as a space of potential realization that does not become extinct in any of its forms: "we surpass ourselves as empirical subjects in order to assume universalizable roles."[42] The transcendental subject is, in this way, deconstructed. After the *egoistic* man (of liberties) and the *situated* man (of the social state), our law, drawing lessons from philosophical analyses, should be able to take into account the theater of human appearances and to offer to the *subject of* stripped of all human depth a juridical transposition.

Non-jurisdiction is not a matter of non-law.[43] On the contrary, it expresses "a point of resistance" which inevitably tends to become a true[44] subject.

The law understood as a mechanism of distance seems to us likely to allow the identification of these mirror effects. In this sense, the now classic question of self-production as a paradox studied by Barel manifests itself in a new form: man produces himself. The *subject* creates the individual, the "non-subject" engenders the person, the communicative act substitutes for the subject and founds him. This duplication, which is the essence of self-production, must be protected.[45] For this, it is appropriate to evoke Roman law and one of its most prestigious and iconoclastic masters.[46] Human society "cannot dispense with putting its subjects in the square."[47] As such, civilization is historically nothing other than the empire of civil

39 It seems obvious that this construction is in debt to the concepts developed by psychoanalysis.

40 See, on this question, the work of Kojève on alienation. A. KOJÈVE, *Introduction à la lecture de Hegel*, Gallimard, 1997.

41 *Cf*, D.-R. Dujour, *Lacan et le miroir sophianique de Boehme*, EPEL, Paris, 1998.

42 A. RENAUT and L. SOSOE,*Philosophy of Law, op. cit.* p. 425.

43 J. CARBONNIER,"Sur les traces du non-sujet de droit." *Archives de philosophie du droit*, 34 (1989), p. 197. On this question, see his analysis of non-subjects revealed by the analysis of personality (the incapable, the indistinguishable), non-subjects revealed by the opposition of the thing to the person, non-subjects revealed by the relation of the person to life, etc., in which the person is the subject of the law.

44 *Idem*, p. 206.

45 As Barel observes, "the fusion and confusion of levels are the daily bread of wild or mythological thought." In this sense, "let us have the mischievousness to observe in passing this paradox, modernity rediscovers one of the basic constants of wild thought and mythology even in its distant extensions: the eye that looks at itself." Y. BAREL, *Le paradoxe et le système*, PUG, Paris, 1989, p. 27. *Cf.* also on the notion of paradox in law: TEUBNER G., "Et Dieu rit...," *APD*, 34 (1989), p. 266 ff.

46 *Cf.* on this question, P. LEGENDRE, *L'inestimable objet de la transmission; Étude* sur le *principe généalogique en Occident*, Fayard, Paris, 1985, p. 9.

47 *Id.* p. 11.

law. Legal fiction (which is therefore only dogmatic: in this sense, dogma makes it possible to make people believe, it is only the discourse of a society on its staged truth), in accordance with social dogmatics, "is the art of establishing legality in order to give birth to, nourish and lead human subjects to death."[48] Law is therefore an art of reproduction, the art of dividing the human being or the art of controlled asymmetry (the genealogy of civil law is the archetype of this art, since it thus distinguishes the multiple ascendants – *pater, mater, avus, avia, proavus, proavia* – descendants – *filius, filia, nepos, neptis, pronepos, proneptis* – and collateral lines[49]). The vocation of the law is to "put at a distance" a reality that the law is only intended to produce[50] as well as possible by means of a technical tool capable of ensuring its "formal realizability" [*Ihering*]. Give in to your desire, obey the law and you will receive as a reward a flood of love, as Legendre states in *The Love of the Censor.*

The question of the subject posed and the search for the non-subject of law conducted, it is naturally to a questioning on the interpreter that we end up. The jurist with regard to the subject heard in its entirety must therefore be present where the demands exist. Faced with the glove turned over, assuming (interpret?) that the hand knew what it was doing, does this not allow it to be restored to a subject in conformity with the needs of an interrogation on the human being?[51] The role of the jurist is therefore to make inhabitable for man the space of representation that he gives to himself by means of legal discourse.

From then on, Gramsci and Althusser evoked on this occasion illustrate, together, the unimpeachable complexity of the individual at grips with normativity.

48 *Id.* p. 13.

49 In this relationship to the other there is a relationship to exteriority that Professor Rials studying Villey's work has perfectly highlighted. In this sense, the law has as its vocation to pronounce on relationships, and for Villey this function makes it possible to ensure the adequate sharing of *res esteriores* (the law empty of content, is the just sharing even outside the exercise of the virtue of justice). The school of "componential analysis," as soon as it makes it possible to relate series of semes, can illustrate the structural logic that we are trying to evoke by highlighting the significant differences between the series A juri-seme thus takes on meaning both by means of a relationship with the set of juri-semes that make up the legal lexicon and with regard to a series derived from the current meaning of the notion.

50 "The subject exists in and by law only to the extent, the exact extent, to which it is inscribed in it and so manifest as to determine a priori its meaning." G. TIMSIT, *Les noms de la loi*, PUF, Paris, 1991, p. 74.

51 In sociology, Alain Touraine's thought process is much the same. This author returns to the notion of the subject, at the end of which the *contemporary subject* distinguishes itself from the *I* (understood as identifications of the person with social roles) and the *Self* (expectations of social roles of the individual) to constitute itself as an *empty subject with* no other content than its effort of reconstruction. It is particularly interesting for the jurist to highlight the fact that for the French sociologist "it must be recognized today that the problems of private life, culture and personality are at the heart of public life." *Cf.* A. TOURAINE, *Critique de la modernité*, Paris, Fayard, 1992, p. 337.

B The standards that govern the delayed appearance of the subject

In this last part, our approach will be pragmatic.[52] It will thus be necessary to conduct an investigation related to the complexity of this differentiated appearance specific to the subject in the order of our society. This appearance must be justified by certain social norms and by a specific rationality. There is, in fact, an agreement on a shared belief about what a subject is and how it should be taken into account socially.

The management in our democracies of the various minorities is particularly illustrative of this question. We can see that in front of the delicate work of a conceptual definition of minorities, the political (and legal) management of this problem is generally based on a more or less subtle displacement of this question. This displacement is achieved through *metaphorical* and *metonymic* effects.

The metaphor thus shifts from minority to minority and the metonymy of minorities to certain minorities (religious, linguistic, etc.[53]). In this sense, the appearance of the subject – minority or minority – is always embodied in the places where it is called to appear. His address in social reality is prior to his incarnation.

What needs to be investigated pragmatically is the rationality of this belief. It is a question of properly questioning this habit of action on the basis of which we would be willing to act. In action (i.e., in the whirlwind of a "form of life") individuals rely on beliefs that form the basis of ideology: they stop questioning the world and rely on a certain apparent certainty and on an agreement implicit in criteria. In law, the translation of this agreement seems to manifest itself in Hart's rules of recognition, as well as in certain so-called constitutive norms, etc., which thus form the blind spot from which law determines the validity inherent in its own order.

Belief is fixed by a rule of action whose rationality is not to be sought beforehand as the cause, but which is retroactively posed as the reason for these behaviors.

So there is a belief about what a subject is. This belief is elaborated in an ideology and it is fixed by a rule of action.

Contemporary belief is thus that of a subject likely to be declined in a series that never exhausts the substance of what it is. The political orientations (and the normativity inherent in it) that are currently linked to sexualities seem particularly paradigmatic of this ideology. The individual would then be the creator of his or her identities and would not accept being placed under house arrest by a symbolic order. He would always be in surplus of it. What is then valued is freedom and this is unfortunately to the detriment of the fact that freedom is never more than the intellection of necessity according to Spinoza's formula.

52 For a presentation of the issues and questions inherent in pragmatism: J.-P. COMETTI, *Qu'est-ce que le pragmatisme*, Gallimard, Paris, 2010.

53 On this question our thesis, *La protection constitutionnelle des minorités en France et en Italie*, Toulon 1998.

The blind spot of this belief (the basis of its truth) remains to be explored, however. If truth is understood to be the order of correspondence (which is generally the common definition) it is obvious that discourse does not give a real access to the world, but only a hold on it. This translates into the formula that language is *in* the world, not *on* it.

The truth wich is inherent in this belief thus lies in the correspondence not of political discourse to an external reality (which would be the world itself), but in the reference from one level of discourse to another level of discourse (according to Tarski's famous 1933 thesis on the T convention). It is about the correspondence between an ordinary discourse and a functional discourse that ensures that certain things can work (politics, which attaches itself to a creative function of the social bond and to the effectiveness of some commandments, and law, which attaches itself to offering a certain confidence in the response to normative expectations[54]). In this second perspective, truth is purely decitative. It is the reception by a speaker of a truth uttered by another speaker. It is part of the agreement *in* discourses present in the world. This approach offers to manifest the blind spot of ideology. If the truth of this belief is expressed in agreement, what is shown is that the correspondence between these discourses offers only two possibilities: either the redundancy expressed is nothing (there is only a tautology, an identical repetition of one discourse by another) or it expresses something whose nature will have to be determined: a simple objective repetition of criteria on which we agree.

Intuitively, however, we know that in the ordinary of a discourse what manifests itself and gives meaning to our purpose is more the place of our enunciation than the semantic meaning of it. What manifests itself in "surplus" is the part of the enunciation that the subject of the utterance always conceals.

The question of the subject in the field of politics and law is thus an illustration not of what the subject itself would be, but of the rationality inherent in the way in which language functions in its relation to the mind and the world. The subject of this relationship is a remnant that never blooms, and ideology seeks to mask this by making the subject someone who runs after this remnant hoping to finally become complete. There is a voice that sometimes struggles to be heard.

54 Here we find the final distinction between law presented as a declination of law and law as an inherent practice of jurisdictions. We find this distinction in the difference between reflexive law and directive law.

Bibliography

Althusser, L. (1994). *Ecrits philosophiques et politiques*, Vol. 1, Livre de poche, Paris.

Althusser, L. and Balibar, E. (1968). *Lire le Capital*, Vol. 1, Maspero, Paris.

Amselek, P. (2012). *Cheminements philosophiques dans le monde du droit et des règles en général*, Armand Colin, Paris.

Amselek, P. (2019). *Écrits de philosophie du droit*, Panthéon-Assas, Paris.

Anne-Braun, A. (2018). *Le monde en projet: Une lecture de la théorie des symboles de Nelson Goodman*, Presse Université Paris Sorbonne, Paris.

Austin, J.-L. (1994). *Écrits philosophiques*, Seuil, Paris.

Azoulai, L. (2013). "La limite à l'arrêt. Positivité de la transgression chez J. Derrida," in *La transgression*, Bruylant, Bruxelles, p. 504.

Badiou, A. (2015). *A la recherche du réel perdu*, Fayard, Paris.

Barel, Y. (1989). *Le paradoxe et le système*, Presse Université Grenoble, Grenoble.

Benoist, J. (2010). *Concepts: Introduction à l'analyse*, Cerf, Paris.

Benoist, J. (2013). *Le bruit du sensible*, Cerf, Paris

Benoist, J. (2015). *Phénoménologie, sémantique, ontologie: Husserl et la tradition logique autrichienne*, PUF, Paris.

Benoist, J. (2017). *L'adresse du réel*, Vrin, Paris.

Benoit, J.P. (1995). "Notions et concepts, instruments of legal knowledge. Les leçons de la philosophie du droit de Hegel," in *Mélanges peiser*, Presse Universitaire Grenoble, Grenoble, p. 27.

Bergson, H. (2007). *L'évolution créatrice*, PUF, Paris.

Bordes, E. (2018). *Le silence et le droit, recherches sur une métaphore*, Presse Universitaire Laval, Québec.

Bourdieu, B. (2012). *Sur l'etat: Cours au collège de France 1989–1992*, Seuil, Paris.

Bousseyroux, M. (2008). "Le pastout: Sa logique et sa topologie," in *L'en-je Lacanien*, 10, pp. 9–27.

Bouveresse, J. (1973). *Wittgenstein: La rime et la raison, science éthique et esthétique*, Editions de minuit, Paris.

Bouveresse, J. (2015). "Les raisons et les causes" in *Philosophie, mythologie et pseudo science, Wittgenstein lecteur de Freud*, 2nd ed., l'Eclat, Paris.

Brandom, R. (2009). *L'articulation des raisons: Introduction à l'inférentialisme*, Cerf, Paris.

Brandom, R. (2010). *Rendre explicite: raisonnement, représentation et engagement discursif*, Cerf, Paris.

Brentano, F. (2008). *Psychologie du point de vue empirique*, Vrin, Paris.

Brunet, P. (2009). "Les juges européens au pays des valeurs," in *La vie des idées*, June,. www.laviedesidees.fr/Les-juges-europeens-au-paysdes.html

Buzzi, A.-R. (1967). *La théorie politique d'Antonio Gramsci*, Nauwelaerts, Louvain.

Caillosse, J. (2015). *L'État du droit administratif*, LGDJ, Paris.

Carbonnier, J. (1989). "Sur les traces du non-sujet de droit," *Archives de philosophie du droit*, 34, p. 197.

Cavaillé, C. (2016). *Les jeux de language chez Wittgenstein*, Demopolis, Paris.

Cavell, S. (1993). *A la recherche du bonheur: Hollywood et la comédie de remariage*, Cahiers du cinéma. Paris.

Cavell, S. (1996). *Wittgenstein: Les voix de la raison, scepticisme moralité et tragédie*, Seuil, Paris.

Cavell, S. (2009). *Dire et vouloir dire*, Cerf, Paris.

Cavell, S. (2009). *Qu'est-ce que la philosophie américaine*, Gallimard, Paris.

Chapus, R. (1966). "De la valeur juridique des principes généraux du droit et des autres règles jurisprudentielles du droit administratif," *Dalloz*, p. 99.

Chaudet, J.P. (1967). "Les principes généraux de la procédure administrative contentieuse," LGDJ, Paris.

Cometti, J.-P. (2010). *Qu'est-ce que le pragmatisme?* Gallimard, Paris.

Conte, A.G. (1986). "Phenomena of phenomena," in *Interpretation and epistemology. Acts of the VII colloquium on interpretation*, Galli, Turin, pp. 167–198.

Conte, A.G. (2001). *Filosofia del linguaggio normativo, III, studi 1995–2001*, Giappichelli, Turin.

Crewe, D. (2013). "Socio-cultural origins of law," in *Transgression and deviance*, Palgrave Macmillan, UK.

Davidson, D. (1993/1984). *Inquiries into truth and interpretation*, tr. P. Engel, Clarendon Press, Oxford, especially on the principle of charity, pp. 267–289.

Defoort, B. (2015). *La décision administrative*, LGDJ, Paris.

Dennett, D. (1993). *La conscience expliquée*, O. Jacob, Paris.

Dennett, D. (2005). *De beaux rêves: Obstacles philosophiques à une science de la conscience*, Gallimard, Paris.

Di Lucia, P. (1997). *L'universale della promessa*, Giuffrè, Milan.

Di Lucia, P. (2003). *Ontologia sociale potere deontico e regole costitutiva*, Quodlibet, Macerata.

Dujour, D.-R. (1998). *Lacan et le miroir sophianique de Boehme*, EPEL, Paris.

Eisenmann, Ch. (1957). "Le droit administratif et le principe de légalité," *EDCE*, Paris.

Favoreu, L. (2000). *Droit des libertés fondamentales*, Dalloz, Paris.

Finnis, J. (1980). *Natural law and natural rights*, Clarendon, Oxford.

Frege, G. (1971). *Écrits logiques et philosophiques*, tr. C. Imbert, Éditions du Seuil, Paris.

Frier, P.-L. and Petit, J. *Droit administratif*, LGDJ, Paris.

Gallerand, A. (2014). *Husserl et le phénomène de la signification*, Vrin, Paris.

Gardies, J.-L. (1972). *Essai sur les fondements a priori de la rationalité morale et juridique*, LGDJ, Paris.

Gardies, J.-L. (1987). *L'erreur de Hume*, PUF, Paris.

Geiger, Th. (1970/1947). *Vorstudien zu einer Soziologie des Rechts*, Munksgaard, Copenhagen.

Glock, H.-J. (2003). *Dictionnaire Wittgenstein, Dictionnaire Wittgenstein*, Gallimard, Paris.

Golding, M.P. (1981). "Realism and functionalism in the legal thoughts of Felix S. Cohen," *Cornell Law Quarterly*, 66 (1032).

Goodman, N. (2006). *Manières de faire des mondes,* Gallimard, Paris.

Gramsci, A. (1974). *Les écrits politiques,* I, 1914–1920, Gallimard, Paris.

Guastini, R. (2010). *Le fonti del diritto. Fondamenti teorici*, Giuffrè, Milano.

Gueroult, M. (1967). *Leibniz: Dynamique et métaphysique*, Aubier, Paris.

Gwynne, J.K. (2016). *Anglo-American cinema: Gender, sex, and the deviant body*, Columbia University Press, New York.

Hart, H.L.A. (1963). *Law, liberty, and morality*, Stanford University Press, Stanford.

Heath, J. (2001). "Brandom and the sources of normativity," *Philosophiques,* 28 (1), p. 29.

Hegel, G.W.F. (1946). *Genèse et structure de la phénoménologie de l'esprit*, Vol. 1, Aubier, Paris.

Kojève, A. (1997). *Introduction à la lecture de Hegel*, Gallimard, Paris.

Koubi, G. (2003). *Les circulaires administratives*, Economica, Paris.

Lachaume, J.L. et al. (2017). *Droit administratif: Les grandes décisions de la jurisprudence*, 17th ed., PUF, Paris.

Lacroix, J. (1971). *Marxisme, existentialisme personnalisme,* PUF, Paris.

Lakoff, G. and Johnson, M. (1985). *Les métaphores dans la vie quotidienne*, Editions de minuit, Paris.

Latour, B. (2002). "Petite philosophie de l'énonciation," *Texto*! 11 (2). www.revue-texto.net/Inedits/Latour_Enonciation.html

Latour, B. (2004). "Notes brèves sur l'écologie du droit saisie comme une énonciation," in *Cosmopolitiques: Pratiques cosmopolitiques du droit, cahiers théoriques pour l'écologie politique*, 8, L'Aube, Paris, pp. 34–40.

Latour, B. (2012). *Enquête sur les modes d'existence: Une anthropologie des modernes,* La Découverte, Paris.

Laugier, S. (2005). "L'importance de l'importance: Expérience, pragmatisme, transcendentalisme," *Multitudes*, 4 (23), pp. 153–167.

Laugier, S. (2011). "Presentation, Stanley Cavell," *Revue internationale de philosophie*, 2, p. 114.

Legendre, P. (1985). *L'inestimable objet de la transmission; étude sur le principe généalogique en Occident*, Fayard, Paris.

Lévi-Strauss, C. (1985). "Les organisations dualiste existent-elles existent-elles?" in *Anthropologie structurale,* Plon, Paris.

Lewis, D. (2007). *De la pluralité des mondes,* tr. M. Caveribère and J.-P. Cometti, Editions de l'éclat, Paris and Tel-Aviv.

Llewellyn, K. (2008). *Jurisprudence. Realism in theory and practice*, Routledge, New York.

Lorenzini, D. (2015). *Éthique et politique de soi: Foucault, Hadot, Cavell et les techniques de l'ordinaire*, Vrin, Paris.

Luciani, M. (2006). "Constitutionalismo irenico e costituzionalismo polemico," in *Giurisprudenza costituzionale*, 2, pp. 1643–1668.

Luhmann, N. (2001) *La légitimation par la procédure*, tr. L.K. Sosoe and S. Bouchard, PUL/Cerf, Paris.

Luhmann, N. (2006). *La confiance. Un mécanisme de réduction de la complexité sociale*, tr. S. Bouchard, Economica, Paris.

Marrani, D. (2015). Reinforcing environmental rights: The French charter for the environment, *Revista Europea de Derechos Fundamentales primer semester*, 25, pp. 383–400.

Marrani, D. (2018). *Space, time, justice*, Routledge, London.

Merleau-Ponty, M. (1964). *Le visible et l'invisible*, Gallimard, Paris.

Millard, E. (2006). *Théorie du droit,* Dalloz, Paris.

Millard, E. (2014). "Qui sont les opérateurs juridiques de R. Guastini," in *Analisi e diritto*, pp. 103–113.

Montminy, M. (2002). "Normativité et irréductibilité du mental," *Dialectica*, 56 (4), p. 317.

Moor, P. (2010). *Dynamique du système juridique: une théorie générale du droit*, Bruylant, LGDJ, Paris.

Morant-Deviller, P.J., Bourdon, P. and Poulet, F. (2017). *Droit administratif*, LGDJ, Paris, p. 392.

Murdoch, I. (2015). *Sartre un rationaliste romantique*, Payot, Paris

Pardini, J.-J. (2002). *Le juge constitutionnel et le fait en Italie*, PUAM, Aix, Marseille.

Passerini Glazel, L. (2005). *La forza normativa del typo, pramgatica dell'atto giuridico e teoria della catagorizzazione*, Quodlibet Studio, Macerata.

Passerini Glazel, L. (2008). "Eidologique et eidonomique dans la philosophie de l'acte juridique: Adolf Reinach et Czeslaw Znamierowski," in *Adolf Reinach entre droit et phénoménologie*, CNRS, Paris, pp. 59–70.

Passerini Glazel, L. (2012). *Atto, norma, tipo: Tra pragmatica e ontologia del diritto*, Aracne, Rome.

Passerini-Glazel, L. (2018). "Les normes vécues et les normes simplement pensées *noema* déontique et expérience normative dans Kelsen, Weber, Petra⊠ycki and Weinberger," in *Sociologie du droit*, 1.

Petta, P. (1975). *Ideologie costituzionali della sinistra italiana (1892–1974)*, Savelli, Rome.

Putnam, H. (1992). *Definitions: Why can't reason be naturalized*, tr. C. Bouchindhomme, L'éclat, Paris.

Putnam, H. (2011). *Le réalisme à visage humain*, Gallimard, Paris.

Quine, W.V. (1993). *La poursuite de la vérité*, tr. M. Clavelin, Seuil, Paris.

Rabachou, J. (2016). *Qu'est-ce qu'un monde?* Vrin, Paris.

Raffestin, C. (2003). "Penser et classer dans les sciences sociales," *Revue Européenne des Sciences Sociales*, 41 (127).

Recanati, F. (1979). *La transparence et l'énonciation*, Seuil, Paris.

Reinach, A. (2004). *Les fondements* a priori *du droit civil*, Vrin, Paris.

Renaudie, J.M. (2006). "L'être et le sens des états de choses: Recherches logiques," in J. Benoist, ed., *Propositions et états de choses: Entre être et sens*, Vrin, Paris, pp. 130–131.

Renaut, A. and Sosoe, L. (1991). *Philosophie du droit*, PUF, Paris.

Revert, M. (2013). "Le droit administratif français et la transgression," in J.J. Sueur and P. Richard, eds, *La transgression*, Bruylant, Paris, pp. 261–282.

Richard P. and Passerini-Glazel, A. (2021). *Anthologie des textes du professeur A. G. Conte: Recherches sur la philosophie du langage normatif*, PUL, Québec.

Rivero J. (1968). "Sur la rétroactivité de la règle jurisprudentielle," *AJDA*, p. 16

Rivero, J. (1951). "Le juge administratif français: Un juge qui gouverne?" *Dalloz*, p. 23.

Romano, C. (2010). *Au cœur de la raison phénoménologique*, Gallimard, Paris, 2010.

Schelling, F.W.J. (1977). *Recherches sur la liberté humaine et les objets qui s'y rattachent*, Payot, Paris.

Sebestik, J. (1922). *Logique et mathématiques chez Bernard Bolzano*, Vrin, Paris.

Sichère, B. (2018). *Aristote au soleil de l'être*, CNRS, Paris

Sueur, J.J. and Richard, P. (2013). *La transgression*, Bruylant, Bruxelles.

Tappolet, Ch. (2011). "La normativité des concepts évaluatifs," *Philosophiques*, 38, pp. 157–176.

Teubner, G. (1989). "Et Dieu rit …, " *APD*, 34, p. 266.

Teubner, G. (1993). *Le droit un système autopoïétique*, tr. G. Maier and N. Boucquey, PUF, Paris.

Texier, J. (1975). "Gramsci in Francia," in *Gramsci e la cultura contemporanea*, Vol. 2, Istituto Gramsci, Rome.

Tiercelin, C. (2011). *Le ciment des choses: Petit traité de métaphysique scientifique réaliste*, Ithaque, Paris.

Timsit, G. (1991). *Les noms de la loi*, PUF, Paris.

Timsit, G. (2000). "La métaphore dans le discours juridique," *Revue européenne des sciences sociales*, 38 (117), pp. 83–94.

Troper, M. (1992). "Sur l'usage des concepts juridiques en histoire," *Annales. Economies, Societies, Civilisations*, 47 (6).

Troper, M. (1994). "Système juridique et État," in *Pour une théorie juridique de l'État*, PUF, Paris, p. 170.

Tugendhat, E. (1995). *Conscience de soi et autodétermination*, Armand Colin, Paris.

Turner, S., Shelton, D., Razzaque, J., McIntyre, O. and May, J. (eds) (2019). *Environmental rights: The development of standards*. Cambridge University Press, Cambridge.

Tusseau, G. (ed.) (2009). *Les notions juridiques. Journée d'étude de la promotion d'agrégation de droit public*, Economica, Aix, Marseille.

Vedel, G. (1948). "De l'arrêt Septfonds à l'arrêt Barinstein (la légalité des actes administratifs devant les juridictions judiciaires)," *JCP*, 1, p. 682.

Wittgenstein, L. (1980). *Bemerkungen über die philosophie der psychologie*, I and II, ed. G.E. M. Anscombe and G.H. von Wright, tr. G. Granel, Blackwell, Oxford, pp. 624–625.

Wittgenstein, L. (2001). *Tractatus logico-philosophicus*, Gallimard, Paris.

Wittgenstein, L. (2004). *Recherches philosophiques*, Gallimard, Paris.

Zanchettin, C. (1972). "L'epistemologia marxista di Louis Althusser," *Il Mulino*, 220, March–April, p. 266.

Zizek, S. (2018). Essai sur Schelling: Le reste qui n'éclot jamais, L'Harmattan, Paris.

Index

For Product Safety Concerns and Information please contact our EU representative GPSR@taylorandfrancis.com
Taylor & Francis Verlag GmbH, Kaufingerstraße 24, 80331 München, Germany

www.ingramcontent.com/pod-product-compliance
Lightning Source LLC
LaVergne TN
LVHW021131300926
849160LV00010B/969

9780367655648